KT-453-841

Penguin Critical Studies
Advisory Editor: Bryan Loughrey

Virginia Woolf

To the Lighthouse

Stevie Davies

CHESTER COLLEGE

ACC. No. DEPT.
00937090

CLASS No.
823.912 WOO
D26

LIBRARY

Penguin Books

PENGUIN BOOKS

Published by the Penguin Group
Penguin Books Ltd, 27 Wrights Lane, London W8 5TZ, England
Viking Penguin, a division of Penguin Books USA Inc.
375 Hudson Street, New York, New York 10014, USA
Penguin Books Australia Ltd, Ringwood, Victoria, Australia
Penguin Books Canada Ltd, 2801 John Street, Markham, Ontario, Canada L3R 1B4
Penguin Books (NZ) Ltd, 182–190 Wairau Road, Auckland 10, New Zealand

Penguin Books Ltd, Registered Offices: Harmondsworth, Middlesex, England

First published 1989
10 9 8 7 6 5 4 3 2

Copyright © Stevie Davies, 1989
All rights reserved

Printed in England by Clays Ltd, St Ives plc
Filmset in Monophoto Times

Except in the United States of America, this book is sold subject
to the condition that it shall not, by way of trade or otherwise, be lent,
re-sold, hired out, or otherwise circulated without the publisher's
prior consent in any form of binding or cover other than that in
which it is published and without a similar condition including this
condition being imposed on the subsequent purchaser

Accession no.
00937090

LIBRARY

Tel: 01244 375444   Ext: 3301

This book is to be returned on or before the
last date stamped below. Overdue charges
will be incurred by the late return of books.

Chester

A College of the
University of Liverpool

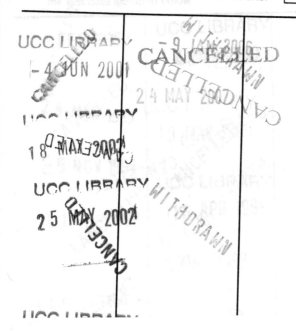

UCC LIBRARY
- 4 JUN 2001

UCC LIBRARY
18 MAY 2002

UCC LIBRARY
25 MAY 2002

UCC LIBRARY

CANCELLED

- 9 MAY 2006

24 MAY 2002

WITHDRAWN

Dr Stevie Davies studied English Literature at Manchester University, where she went on to lecture from 1971 to 1984. She left teaching to become a full-time novelist and literary critic. Her novel *Boy Blue* was published by the Woman's Press in 1987, and her other publications include *Emily Brontë: The Artist as a Free Woman* (Carcanet Press, 1983), *Images of Kingship in Paradise Lost* (University of Missouri Press, 1983), *The Idea of Woman in Renaissance Literature* (Harvester, 1986) and *Emily Brontë* in the Harvester 'Key Women Writers' series, 1988.

Contents

To Frank
It partook, she felt . . .
of eternity

Acknowledgements and Bibliographical Note

The origins of this book lie in an Extra-Mural course I led at the University of Manchester entitled 'Only Connect: Novels by Virginia Woolf and E. M. Forster' in Spring 1988. I should like to thank all the members of that group for their memorable perceptions and thoughts so freely shared: I think each will find in my book traces of herself or himself, still recognizable, though partly dissolved in the common pool of thought we created and on which I have gratefully drawn. I consider this book as a tribute to them.

I must thank my dear friend William Hunter, Professor Emeritus in English Literature at the University of Houston, not only for his wisdom and the grace of his conversation but also for the more tangible gifts of Virginia Woolf's diaries, essays and stories in beautiful hard-cover volumes for my shelves. He will recognize everywhere between these covers the fruit of his kindness.

I thank Rosalie Wilkins for her unfailing support and encouragement during the writing of the book, and Andrew Howdle for many wonderful conversations on Modernism.

To facilitate ease of reference for students, where possible I have referred to all cited works in accessible editions, and principally in Penguin editions, especially the novels of Virginia Woolf, George Eliot, E. M. Forster, and the works of Plato and the Greek pastoralists. I have, however, used the edition of *To the Lighthouse* that is published in paperback by Grafton.

S.D.
August 1988

1. The Field of Vision

Virginia Woolf had just been born when her father, Leslie Stephen, wandering Cornwall in the spring of 1882, came upon St Ives Bay, was captivated by its beauty and founded there one of his daughter's primal memories. Talland House which he rented for his family was the sanctuary to which summer by summer for the next ten years the family migrated. It was less a holiday home than an alternative world, full of paradisal refreshment. St Ives mysteriously carried the meaning of her childhood for Virginia Woolf, in its threefold conjunction of sea, the acreage of garden sloping down to the sea, and the house itself embracing the presences of her parents. In *To the Lighthouse*, St Ives is translated into the Hebridean island where the Ramsays have their refuge. The garden becomes the palimpsest upon which Mr Ramsay, circling in his customary round of meditation, mentally inscribes his thought processes upon every familiar leaf and flower-pot; Talland House is memorialized as the interior world of the presiding mother who sits at its window and sheds her own mental light on the eye of the equally presiding lighthouse; and the sea is everywhere – it is 'to be heard all through [the novel]', as Virginia Woolf recorded in her diary (*Diary*, III, p. 34). The sea as originally heard and viewed from Talland House is the essence of the work's symbolic structure. The element of birth and death that remembers the sea-changes of Shakespeare's Last Plays, Milton's *Lycidas*, Cowper's *The Castaway*, Arnold's *Marguerite*, it is at once a chaotic realm whose formlessness figures all that human beings most fear in the universe, an apocalyptic Flood and the rhythmic cradle and lullaby of Being.

The Eden whose forfeit Milton records in *Paradise Lost* was lost to Virginia Woolf after the Stephen family abdicated their retreat under the shadow of the growing commercialization of the area. After the Great War, she and her sister Vanessa stole back and peered over the wall at the new owners' property; in late middle age she again returned under cover of darkness and stared with unassuaged grief into the desecrated sanctuary of her long-dead parents. *To the Lighthouse* was one of the most personal and emotional books Virginia Woolf ever wrote, and one of the easiest to write, save that her thoughts flew too swiftly ahead of her pen and she had to race along in their wake. She was still in process of finishing *Mrs Dalloway* (1925) when the idea for the new work dawned, and she longed to lay aside the more laborious and exacting work in favour of the new inspiration. On 14 May 1925 she recorded in her diary that she was:

now all on the strain with desire . . . to get on to *To the Lighthouse*. This is going to be fairly short: to have father's character done complete in it; & mother's; & St Ives; & childhood; & all the usual things I try to put in – life, death &c. But the centre is father's character, sitting in a boat, reciting We perished each alone, while he crushes a dying mackerel – However, I must refrain. (*Diary*, III, pp. 18–19)

As she wrote, her pen was to edge the portrait of the father out of the centre of the picture and, indeed, to diffuse the centre altogether into a pool of consciousness whose centre, like that of the medieval God, is everywhere and whose circumference nowhere. Mr Ramsay does put out to sea in the fisherman's boat, does recite Cowper's *Castaway*, and a mutilated mackerel with a square cut out of it for bait is thrown back into the sea still living, to perish alone with the rest of the animal creation – but this is all placed in the closing phase of the novel. All the other predicted ingredients, however, are there in the final work: mother, childhood, 'life, death &c.' But two distinct kinds of portraiture emerged within the narrative span of the novel, the one suggested by the vignette of Mr Ramsay's unusual behaviour in the boat, the other involving all that is implied in the term 'stream of consciousness'.

Mr Ramsay is focused chiefly from without, behaviourally, and we enter into him only fleetingly and generally without feeling that his unique 'eye-beam' is one that will yield us very much personal light; Mrs Ramsay is a diffused thinking presence which is indwelling throughout the novel, as much after her death as before, when the universe becomes, as Emily Brontë's Heathcliff says of the world without Catherine, 'a dreadful collection of memoranda that she did exist, and that I have lost her' (*Wuthering Heights*, Ch. 33). It is as if Virginia Woolf needed to exorcize the daemon of her father, with his tantrums, exhibitionism and diabolical extortions of support and sympathy from women, by focusing him in a caricature of truly Dickensian proportions. Yet the caricature is delicately made, so that it swims in an ocean of Virginia Woolf's ambivalent irony. This irony communicates a double attitude, both of ridicule and regard, anger and pity. She portrayed her father in general from the outside both because, in his determined egocentric otherness, he had resisted assimilation, and because, even decades after his death, he was a thorn in her flesh which she needed to extrude. The narrative voice of *To the Lighthouse* fuses with the mother-consciousness and dissects away the father-consciousness. 'One wanted', thinks Lily Briscoe, 'fifty pairs of eyes to see with' (p. 182), and James, on the boat with his silently reading parent and his haze of memories of his mother and the happy world of childhood, realizes that 'nothing was simply one thing' (p. 172). *To the Lighthouse* teaches us that, if fifty pairs of eyes may be considered an extravagant requirement, we need and can manage to produce at least two pairs each. The book attributes integrity to double vision. Mr Ramsay is to Cam both tyrant and beloved, ridiculous and insulting petty dictator and estimable spirit. Both perspectives must be held to be true in the tempering comic world in which the narrative persona adjudicates, condemns to our ridicule but commends to our love. The father who was Virginia Woolf's author becomes the author's creature, to curse and bless; thus fiction both takes revenge for reality and by adjusting perspectives forgives, calms, pays tribute and asks pardon. *To the Lighthouse* is most deeply a novel concerned with perspectives. Just as *Mrs Dalloway* should be read with a map of London at one hand and a striking clock at the other (the novel's bearings being dictated by the relation between the two), *To the Lighthouse* seems to indicate a handy theodolite or sextant to measure its complex geometry of discrepant eye-beams.

We know Mr Ramsay by his boots, by the pudding-basin into which his hair is cut, by the earwig in his milk. We hear his voice in his sallies up and down the terrace and garden roaring *The Charge of the Light Brigade* to the great alarm of his house-guests and, in Part Three, lugubriously intoning Cowper's *Castaway* while his offspring mutely grind their teeth. The scrupulous work of drawing the sting of paternal tyranny is accomplished by these comic deflations; but simultaneously the work of love and restitution is performed by exposing his human vulnerableness through the stooping of his greatness to such details. Mr Ramsay is the archetype of the Father as is Mrs Ramsay of the Mother: the old man in the boat on his lonely odyssey, going home, stern, kind, odd, impossible, unfathomable, is mythologized in Virginia Woolf's account into a Wise Fool with his own strange splendour. He was 'shabby, and simple, eating bread and cheese' (p. 189); deep in his book, he begs no surrenders, is venerable and unknowable both to the vigilant girl and to us as readers; and is mysterious both in his inwardness, his 'stream of consciousness' quite undisclosed, and in his curiously meaningful but uninterpretable gestures, raising his right hand unconsciously in the air and letting it fall 'as if he were conducting some secret symphony' (p. 173). Mr Ramsay on the boat with his little company bears cryptic resemblance to King Lear on the heath, both king and fool in the one body. *To the Lighthouse* is at once a joke at Virginia Woolf's father's expense and a tribute to his nobility. The year after the novel came out, she wrote in her diary:

Father's birthday. He would have been [1928 – 1832 = 96] 96, yes, today; & could have been 96, like other people one has known; but mercifully was not. His life would have entirely ended mine. What would have happened? No writing, no books; – inconceivable. I used to think of him & mother daily; but writing The Lighthouse, laid them in my mind. And now he comes back sometimes, but differently. (I believe this to be true – that I was obsessed by them both, unhealthily; & writing of them was a necessary act.) He comes back now more as a contemporary. I must read him some day. I wonder if I can feel again, I hear his voice, I know this by heart? (*Diary*, III, p. 208)

This passage recognizes the degree to which Virginia Woolf's father was experienced as a threat to her independence and creative authority. Freud the patriarch attributed only to the boy-child identification with and aggression against the father, in competition for the mother; the girl-child, identifying with the mother, is supposed to covet the father. But Virginia Woolf and, it is to be supposed, a majority of aspiring, gifted daughters in our society, take the paternal model and have to fight for their lives against its autocracy. For Virginia Woolf her father, a writer and thinker like herself, a gargantuan child rivalling her for mother-love, was a version of the self; her elusive mother the eternal love-object, Rilke's *ewige Weibliche* which she herself could never be and at heart did not desire to be. But if she turned herself around and faced her father from the position of the mother, then he in turn became the love-object. *To the Lighthouse*, true to its double perspectives, mediates both these alternatives, exhibiting the feelings of Elektra in Cam and those of Oedipus in James: it is part of the work's unique wholeness that it is able to inhabit both these states of mind, with something of the androgynous sensibility which she commends in *A Room of One's Own*. James at six years 'hated him . . . He hated him . . . he hated him' (p. 38) and stood ramrod-stiff between his mother's legs in antagonism to the tyrant. Cam's ire at her oppressor's preposterous licence, 'his legs twisted, frowning and fidgeting, and pishing and pshawing' (p. 152) is subverted by passionate tenderness, 'this pressure and division of feeling, this extraordinary temptation' (p. 158). The author who thanked heaven on her father's 96th birthday that he had not lived to see it was a version of James, not Cam, though Cam's authentic accents may be heard in the second of the diary paragraphs, in the musing, melting 'I must read him some day . . .'

The portrait of Virginia Woolf's mother as Mrs Ramsay is the indwelling spirit of the novel. She dominates, or rather blends most diffusely with the narrative voice to mediate, the first Part; her loss is the first and catastrophic disaster in the second; her vanished being is the corporate focus of longing in the final phase – Cam, James, Mr Ramsay, Lily all yearn back with greater or lesser degrees of awareness to her integrating presence, the gap in creation. Virginia Woolf's mother died in 1895, when Virginia was thirteen, precipitating the first of her breakdowns: mother-love, death and anguishing loss of something intrinsic to her own survival were from that day bound in a hopeless knot at the core of her emotional life. *To the Lighthouse* is a testament to the depth and longevity of that bereavement; it carries its light into the tomb of grief and shines it inquiringly upon the imagined eyes of the dead woman. For Mrs Ramsay the third stroke of the lighthouse beam 'seemed to her like her own eyes meeting her own eyes' (p. 61), and just so the lucid eyes of Julia Stephen's daughter sweep back along the rhythms of the novel's prose to reflect upon her mirroring likeness. Virginia Woolf had never during her mother's life thought of her as a distinct personality like her father: rather she was a presence in the home which dissipated itself through every detail and informed the matrix of the children's life with meaning. Hence the diffusive characterization of Mrs Ramsay in *To the Lighthouse*: she is an aura, a pool of being, a thought-process with which the narrative voice alternately fuses and from which it falls away, without obvious thresholds. For Lily, Mrs Ramsay is the bearer of hieroglyphic secrets, in the chambers of whose mind and heart 'were stood, like the treasures in the tombs of kings, tablets bearing sacred inscriptions, which if one could spell them out would teach one everything, but they would never be offered openly, never made public' (p. 50). *To the Lighthouse* tries to supply the art to read these illegible texts, to mingle its voice with the lost voice 'like waters poured into one jar', seeking unity with the unifier. But Lily's metaphor of the tombs with sacred inscriptions is unconsciously funerary. *To the Lighthouse* resembles a literary seance, with the artist as medium seeking communication with the dead.

Throughout the 1920s, Virginia Woolf was bound up with the special beauty and mystery of a woman's love for women, both as mother-figure and as lover. The diary of 1925 charts not only the progress of *To the Lighthouse* but also the ebb and flow of her evolving relationship with Vita Sackville-West, certainly the most passionate attachment of her life which she was to celebrate in her next novel, the fantasia *Orlando*. She distinguishes herself against Vita in revealing terms, for Vita is:

in short (what I have never been) a real woman . . . lavishes on me the maternal protection which, for some reason, is what I have always most wished from everyone. What L[eonard] gives me, & Nessa gives me, & Vita, in her more clumsy external way, tries to give me. (*Diary*, III, p. 52)

Not only her friend's and sister's but also her husband's love are perceived as maternal, immunizing, and consolatory in nature: they do not stint or calculate affections but 'lavish' their gifts upon her, infinitely solacing her infinite vulnerability. For three decades, up to the writing of *To the Lighthouse*, Virginia Woolf had been accompanied by the spectral figure of her mother, hearing her voice, seeing her characteristic gestures and mannerisms. The novel exorcizes this ghost. Casting Julia Stephen forth on the page in fictionalized form, it memorialized, criticized and bounded her in art's containment. In Part One it let her live on the page in all her vitality, beauty and power, guessing her out at the deepest levels, suggesting, exploring, impersonating; in Part Two it ritualized and exorcized her death by turning loss into apocalypse; in Part Three it assented to this death and gradually let her go in formal gestures of renunciation, accompanied by the consolation of symbolism implying the transformation and awakening of the dead. The work defies the rules and expectations associated with the genre of the realistic novel. It is, in the deepest and most precise sense, an elegy, containing all the classic features of elegy: testament to the dead, visits of mourners, questioning of the coherence both of art and the universe in the light of mortality, pastoral (and, in this case, piscatory) association, spirit of place, and cyclical motion toward a final consolation. This is made explicit in the Diary:

I have an idea that I will invent a new name for my books to supplant 'novel'. A new—by Virginia Woolf. But what? Elegy? (*Diary*, III, p. 34)

As early as 1908 she had flamboyantly announced 'how I shall re-form the novel' (*Letters*, I, p. 356). When, nearly twenty years later, she tentatively introduces a generic title for her experiments from *Jacob's Room* to *To the Lighthouse*, it is striking that her Modernism is viewed in the light of an ancient and ritualized tradition of poetry, for which certain methods and rules had been evolved from Theocritus in the third century BC, through Virgil, Spenser, Milton, Shelley, Arnold, Tennyson. The radical part of her procedure in writing that 'elegy', *To the Lighthouse*, then, lies in the transformation of a prose medium to a poetic composition, using the fixities and definites of a classically-based form to interpret the volatility of modern perceptions. In this respect, Virginia Woolf's Modernism is directly comparable with that of the neo--classicist, H D, the inheritor of Sappho. To name her novels 'elegies' is to offer us, as I shall show (see pp. 100 ff.), clues as to how to read them.

To the Lighthouse was written with great speed and ease – 'I am blown like an old flag by my novel . . . writing as fast & freely as I have written in the whole of my life; more so – 20 times more so – than any novel yet' (*Diary*, III, p. 59). The Diary throughout the period of composition of the first draft records a continuous experience of creative joy, the novel pouring from her more fluently than her pen could take her mind's dictation. From the first she knew that 'the sea is to be heard all through it' (*Diary*, III, p. 34), and that is true in every sense. Spirit of place is shared between land and sea, the reader's eye being recurrently directed across the waters to the lighthouse. Part Three apportions the theatre of action between land and sea, the family afloat on their little craft looking back while Lily onshore looks out towards them. The sea thus becomes a field of vision, which eye-beams constantly scan. It comes to represent the whole vista of meditation, a pool or reservoir of thought, upon whose margins Mr Ramsay stands in Part One, at the edge of the cultivable security of the family garden and tries his mind 'on a spit of land which the sea is slowly eating away' (p. 44), and upon whose shore Nancy builds a world in a rock-pool, playing Jehovah to the tiny fish, and Minta loses a precious brooch. For Mrs Ramsay at her dinner-party, the sea presses up against the very window-pane, as the candle-light illumines and seals the room, an inchoate, non-human watery abyss:

for the night was now shut off by panes of glass, which, far from giving any accurate view of the outside world, rippled it so strangely that here, inside the room, seemed to be order and dry land; there, outside, a reflection in which things wavered and vanished, waterily. (p. 91)

Noah's Flood and the Last Judgement of an insanely malign God are implied by the nightmare face of the sea-symbolism in *To the Lighthouse*. The holidaying family has built its frail-walled sanctuary at the edge of a lethal cauldron of destruction. Part Two records the desecration of their Temple by the salty airs that nose like purposive predatory creatures around their home, corrupting and rotting the human interior. But this process has already begun in Part One: the children 'bring the beach in with them' (p. 30) in the form of a trove of fish, crabs, seaweed, shells, and won't wipe their feet, and won't shut doors, as Mrs Ramsay fumes, so that the furniture, books and wall-paper rot with the sea-damps. The sea in *To the Lighthouse* thus becomes assimilated to the Sea of Death, a motif reinforced by the Apocalypse of Part Two with its threefold family death and the holocaust of the Great War. Here the sea is a bloodstained, curdled mirror for human narcissism, beside which insomniac questors stroll seeking answers to the great philosophical questions and receive in reply nothing but terrible, meaningless self-images. Yet as the symbolism builds in the novel, it becomes archetypal and full of double meaning. The novel's Sea of Death is also the Sea of Life, from whose decomposition of what it swallows intimations of new birth arise. Cam's hand trails in the water as the boat sails out,

as her mind made the green swirls and streaks into patterns and, numbed and shrouded, wandered in imagination in that underworld of waters where the pearls stuck in clusters to white sprays, where in the green light a change came over one's entire mind and one's body shone half transparent enveloped in a green cloak. (p. 169)

The passage bears remembrances of Marvell's 'green thought in a green shade' of *The Garden*

> Mean while the Mind, from pleasure less,
> Withdraws into its happiness:
> The Mind, that Ocean where each kind
> Does streight its own resemblance find;
> Yet it creates, transcending these,
> Far other Worlds, and other Seas;
> Annihilating all that's made
> To a green Thought in a green Shade.
>   (*The Garden*, 41–8)

and the 'sea-change' of Shakespeare's 'Full fathom five' elegy in *The Tempest:*

> Full fathom five thy father lies;
>   Of his bones are coral made:

Those are pearls that were his eyes:
　　Nothing of him that doth fade,
But doth suffer a sea-change
Into something rich and strange.
Sea-nymphs hourly ring his knell:
　　　　　[*Burden*: ding-dong.
Hark! now I hear them, – ding-dong, bell.
　　　　(*The Tempest*, I. ii. 394–401)

Cam's imagination streams out into a green sea of reflection, finding a Marvellian pacific happiness in travelling into a boundless, aqueous world which strangely mirrors and refracts the one she carries within. The Platonist conception that knowledge is always and only a matter of recognition (*Meno*, 82a) – that we carry from before our nativity the abstract forms of all that exists in the outside world – lies behind both Marvell's and Virginia Woolf's meditation. The sea without is answered by the sea within: 'the Mind, that Ocean'. In Cam's beautiful 'green' passage of thought the one flows out into the other: yet transforms and recreates what it finds in the 'underworld of waters', just as Marvell's contemplative, soliloquizing spirit recreates the whole universe upon which it muses, 'Annihilating all that's made . . .' Such lyric transformation of the raw material of thought absorbs the soul in a state of jubilant peace – a prelude, of course, to artistic creativity. Cam's spirit moves like the Dove of Genesis upon the face of the waters and creates a visionary world in which suffering, loss and ugliness are transfigured. Her mortal father, accompanying her in the boat, broods upon the pages of his private book. The allusion to Shakespeare's 'Full fathom five' and its 'pearls that were his eyes', reimagined as 'pearls stuck in clusters to white sprays', intimates recovery of an incorruptible version of the father, immersed within her own seas of thought; and, in clothing the reflected image of Cam herself in the 'green cloak' associated with the fertile person of her dead mother, implies the possibility of new birth as her father's and her mother's child. A decade before, Mrs Ramsay quenched her night-fears by covering the skull James insisted on keeping on the nursery wall with her green cloak, and telling enthralling stories to put the little girl to sleep; Cam's mind in reverie mimes that trance-like sliding into creative oblivion. Story-telling for Virginia Woolf is the mothers' gift to the daughters: 'we think back through our mothers'. *To the Lighthouse* presents lyrical images of rebirth by the baptismal and blessing sea. At the same time, the allure of the cold underwater world in which Cam's mind is 'numbed and

9

shrouded' retains its deathward suggestions. The novel constantly recalls to our minds, through its densely allusive textures, renovating stories of rebirth by water – Jonah's retrieval from the whale's belly; the musician Arion salvaged by dolphins – figuring the human sense of a mothering benignity in the Sea of Life. But it balances this intimation by its Modernist revision of sea-pastoral, recognizing Nature's indifference to mortal desire and pathos, recalling to our minds cold stories of sea-seduction – mermaids, Siren song, the Lorelei. It is very hard as we read quite to forget that Virginia Woolf chose to die by water.

In *A Sketch of the Past*, composed in 1939, two years before her suicide, Virginia Woolf recorded her earliest memories. They speak of primal joy, the residue of a pre-historic and pre-verbal condition of amity with the external world, its circumference being the figure of the mother or the talismanic bounding view of an enclosure which reproduced her shelter:

the first memory.

   This was of red and purple flowers on a black ground – my mother's dress; and she was sitting either in a train or in an omnibus, and I was on her lap. I therefore saw the flowers she was wearing very close; and can still see purple and red and blue, I think against the black; they must have been anemones, I suppose. Perhaps we were going to St Ives ... for that will lead to my other memory, which also seems to be my first memory, and in fact it is the most important of all my memories. If life has a base that it stands upon, if it is a bowl that one fills and fills and fills – then my bowl without a doubt stands upon this memory. It is of lying half asleep, half awake, in bed in the nursery at St Ives. It is of hearing the waves breaking, one, two, one, two, behind a yellow blind. It is of hearing the blind draw its little acorn across the floor as the wind blew the blind out It is of lying and hearing this splash and seeing this light, and feeling, it is almost impossible that I should be here; of feeling the purest ecstasy I can conceive. (*Moments of Being*, pp. 74–5)

'If life has a base ... if it is a bowl ...', she hazards in this haunting meditation, then the foundation for the vessel – or cornucopia – of the self rests upon primal memory. The reader of *To the Lighthouse* may go on to muse that, if this novel has a base, if it too is a bowl that is filled and filled with thought and sensation, then it too stands upon primal memory. The child's-eye close-up view of the mother's bodice as a zone of flowers, perused with infinite satisfaction by the becalmed eyes of the young Virginia calls to mind the floral associations of Mrs Ramsay, presiding like Flora over the garden-world of springtime lives and dying as the season mellows. Contemplating 'the dahlias in the big bed, and wondering what about next year's flowers' (p. 64), lamenting her husband's blank imperviousness to the beauty of flowers (p. 67), noting in Lily's favour that 'Lily is so fond of flowers' (p. 97), Mrs Ramsay's person is by delicate, stealthy process of allusion assimilated to that of the Lady of Flowers, inviting worship like a personage scarcely of human clay. She is a regnant queen who solicits homage: even the 'atheist Charles Tansley' with his little grace and great reluctance adores her thus:

all at once he realized that it was this: it was this: – she was the most beautiful person he had ever seen.

With stars in her eyes and veils in her hair, with cyclamen and wild violets – what nonsense was he thinking? She was fifty at least; she had eight children. Stepping through fields of flowers and taking to her breast buds that had broken and lambs that had fallen; with the stars in her eyes and the wind in her hair – He took her bag. (p. 18)

The defensive bathos which deflates Tansley's unaccustomed romantic flight by dumping the high-flown sentence in a 'bag' may remonstrate with its own whimsy and call attention to the conventional elements that ground his fantasies in his own imperfect eloquence ('stars in her eyes ... wind in her hair') but only serves to secure the mythic associations which the entire novel will develop, with the restorative springtime protector of the young of all species (Charles's buds and lambs). Mrs Ramsay is the mother of a Rose and the beloved of a Lily – the Venusian flower of passion and the virginal flower of purity and death. Her daughter Cam, abbreviated from Camilla, picks up the whiteness of Lily's emblem. Virginia Woolf read her own name allegorically, translated it to Lily and spread the mirroring imagery to Cam – Camilla being the name Leonard Woolf gave to his fictional representation of Virginia as untouchable virgin in his early novel, *The Wise Virgins* (1914). The mother's children in *To the Lighthouse* cannot emulate her rich fecundity: like Prue they are stricken in childbirth, deflowered by the god of the underworld who raped the maiden Persephone in a myth that most deeply underlies this novel (see pp. 106 ff.); like Lily they espouse art not nature. Charles's fantasy of Mrs Ramsay as decked with 'cyclamen and wild violets' – red and purple of passion and blood – looks forward across pools of such violent colour to Lily's sacrificial vision of Mrs Ramsay stepping out across the Elysian Fields in the penultimate moments of the novel:

raising to her forehead a wreath of white flowers with which she went. Lily squeezed her tubes again. She attacked that problem of the hedge. It was strange

11

how clearly she saw her, stepping with her usual quickness across fields among whose folds, purplish and soft, among whose flowers, hyacinths or lilies, she vanished. It was some trick of the painter's eye. For days after she had heard of her death she had seen her thus, putting her wreath to her forehead and going unquestionably with her companion, a shadow, across the fields. (p. 168)

With her white wreath of flowers (lilies?) the lady's person resembles a Pre-Raphaelite representation of the Bride of Death: for the recessional figure is equally bridal and funerary. The style of the vision is curiously at odds with the Modernist, abstract and impressionist manner in which Lily paints her own pictures – being neo-classicist and archaic, and belonging, in fact, to the dominant style of the author's childhood, the manner of William Morris and Burne-Jones. Its hyacinths recall the raped youth Hyacinthus, whose story along with the analogous stories of Narcissus and Persephone are braided into the tapestry of *To the Lighthouse* as myths of loss and transformation. The field of flowers across which Lily pictures Mrs Ramsay as moving has just such a tapestried, embroidered or printed feel, familiar in Pre-Raphaelite technique where paint is made to simulate the effects and perspectives of needlework. But perhaps most emotively of all, those 'folds, purplish and soft' may suggest the material of a mother's dress printed with 'purple and red and blue' anemones: the first of the two primal memories upon which Virginia Woolf saw her whole life as founded.

The second and more crucial of Virginia Woolf's primal memories (see p. 10) of lying 'hearing the waves breaking, one, two, one, two, behind a yellow blind' is explicitly echoed in *To the Lighthouse*. This memory seems to have represented the essence of prelapsarian splendour in peacefulness and belonging: 'the feeling, as I describe it sometimes to myself, of lying in a grape and seeing through a film of semi-transparent yellow' (*A Sketch of the Past*, p. 76). Her 1939 memoir conjures us back into a charmed nursery world of pure Being. The lull of its rhythms – 'It is of lying ... It is of hearing', 'one, two, one, two', 'hearing this splash, seeing this light ... ecstasy' – rocks the mind with cradle motion upon its symmetries and reiterations. Light is transformed into a dense glow through a sac of diaphanous yellow; sound is regulated by the consolatory hush of waves and by the blind-acorn's small sound, measuring recurrent not linear Time. There is a sense of pre-conscious blessedness. The elderly woman reinhabits her girlhood, lying as the embryo in its womb, a seeing seed within its grape. The extraordinary image of the occult world of the inside of a grape lets us as readers share the flight of the spirit to the tiny enclosure of safe containment, a Lilliputian largeness of vision which resembles, but is anodyne to, Hamlet's nightmarish fearfulness of the womb: 'I could be bounded in a nutshell, and count myself king of infinite space, were it not that I have bad dreams' (*Hamlet*, II. ii. 264–6). Virginia Woolf's remembrance seems to emulate a pre-birth experience, with the wave-noise recapitulating the soughing of maternal blood in the immersed ear of the unborn, and the 'semi-transparent yellow' recalling the dim suffusion of light that is said to penetrate to the infant's recess. This experience seems to represent the state of Grace for Virginia Woolf, Paradise before its defloration, but reversing the Biblical model, forswearing the Father's prohibitive garden in favour of the Mother's licit retreat.

In *To the Lighthouse*, the memorial image of the yellow blind is given to James, focusing blurry wisps of vision of a pristine world before the Fall, which he conceives as seeing a wagon-wheel ignorantly crush someone's foot in some Edenic garden whose whereabouts in time and space is uncertain:

But whose foot was he thinking of, and in what garden did all this happen? For one had settings for these scenes; trees that grew there; flowers; a certain light; a few figures. Everything tended to set itself in a garden where there was none of this gloom and none of this throwing of hands about; people spoke in an ordinary tone of voice. They went in and out all day long. There was an old woman gossiping in the kitchen; and the blinds were sucked in and out by the breeze; all was blowing, all was growing; and over all those plates and bowls and tall brandishing red and yellow flowers a very thin yellow veil would be drawn, like a vine leaf, at night. Things became stiller and darker at night. But the leaf-like veil was so fine that lights lifted it, voices crinkled it; he could see through it a figure stooping, hear, coming close, going away, some dress rustling, some chain tinkling.
It was in this world that the wheel went over the person's foot . . . (pp. 171–2)

Perhaps no passage more exquisitely demonstrates the fact that Virginia Woolf's mature art concerns not the objects of vision in themselves but an investigation into the means of perception: the gap which intervenes between self and other, subject and object. *To the Lighthouse* looks at people in the act of looking. It examines the individual's eye-beam and reflects upon the colour of the personal light which leads one to interpret the self and the world in a certain way. Here James's inner eye-beam plays back over his entire conscious life-span and shines upon the shadowy presences in a lost world which he can hardly remember but which we as readers have the advantage of knowing intimately. He

13

finds there suggestions for a story – his own life-story – certain indeterminate but meaningful figures, as in a folk-tale, a fresh and fertile setting, and above all the diaphanous veiling of the yellow blind which imparts its colour to the entire field of vision. The blind is mediated as a protective membrane over reality, 'a vine leaf', 'a leaf-like veil'. The image has an extraordinary organic delicacy and transparency, like the very finest of fine eye-lids; so tender, on the very edge of the incorporeal, that bodiless 'lights lifted it, voices crinkled it', the verbal music of dense alliteration and assonance conveying with magical suggestiveness the drowsy, safe strangeness of a child's world seen, perhaps, through its eyelashes half-way between asleep and awake, or through the ear alone as the child subsides to sleep and registers the watch being kept by his mother as she checks on him, through the rustle of her dress and her chain tinkling as she bends above him. Our minds return to Part One, whose epitaph this is, and one of Virginia Woolf's most matchless sentences: 'The house seemed full of children sleeping and Mrs Ramsay listening; of shaded lights and regular breathing' (p. 49).

It is a curious thought that Virginia Woolf's lament for lost childhood and pre-conscious oblivion, for all the avant garde modernity of her manner, represents a development of Victorian sensibility. But perhaps at this distance of over half a century it is possible for us to recognize all Modernism's deep-rootedness in Victorianism, its iconoclastic manifestos and radical techniques (collage, abstraction, stream of consciousness) a magnificent corporate subterfuge covering a malaise inadmissibly Tennysonian and melancholic. 'Murmur of maternal lamentation', 'Inexplicable splendour of Ionian white and gold' (T. S. Eliot, *The Waste Land*, V. 367, III. 265), 'Empty are the ways,/Empty are the ways of this land . . .' (' "Ione, Dead The Long Year" '): Eliot and Pound could out-Tennyson the laureate at will. Eliot's *The Waste Land* and Tennyson's *Ulysses* are equally backward-looking dirges for mythologies now sapless and dejected; the questor is the elegist and mourns his own demise. Indeed a predominant mode both in Victorian and modernist art is elegiac and funerary. The generation whose art matured in the 1920s was born in the 1880s, and betrays much evidence of the terminal sorrow which Victorians wore as a kind of cheerful and edifying blight. The same spirit built Queen Victoria's neo-Gothic sarcophagus for Prince Albert at Windsor, proliferated orgiastic death-bed scenes in novels and popularized *In Memoriam*. Tennyson's Platonism with its yearning for return to the One is also a frank longing for Mother, a reluctant valediction to wordless oblivion:

> The baby new to earth and sky,
>> What time his tender palm is prest
>> Against the circle of the breast,
> Has never thought that 'this is I:'
>
> But as he grows he gathers much,
>> And learns the use of 'I' and 'me,'
>> And finds 'I am not what I see,
> And other than the things I touch.'
>
> So rounds he to a separate mind
>> From whence clear memory may begin,
>> As through the frame that binds him in
> His isolation grows defined.
>> (*In Memoriam*, XLV. st. 1–3)

Evidently Tennyson knew all too well the Woolfian hunger for re-encapsulation in 'the grape'. He regrets the weaning process from the 'circle of the breast' into the closed circle of language which charts the closing of the fontanelle in the dome of the baby's skull. Virginia Woolf and her generation threw over Victorianism but could not so readily expel the Tennyson that was in their blood because they had ingested it with their mothers' milk.

The Diary shows that, with her customary hypercritical insight, Virginia Woolf recognized the Victorian character of the raw material and some of the attitudes in *To the Lighthouse*. In July 1925 she was agitated as to whether 'this theme may be sentimental; father & mother & child in the garden' (*Diary*, III, p. 36), but she relied on the impersonal manner of the central section, with its challenge to old-fashioned assumptions about unity of design, to camouflage this quality. A year later, with the book nearing completion, she was still hazarding, 'I don't feel sure what the stock criticism will be. Sentimental? Victorian?' (p. 107). Even the term she coins for her revolutionary experiments in novel-writing, 'elegy', hearkens back to the Victorian necropolis of mourning poetry, commemorative civic and private statuary, urns and blanched marmoreal guardian angels in much-visited graveyards. The *mater dolorosa* who was the prototype for Mrs Ramsay was herself a relict. In a sense Virginia Woolf's birth was posthumous, since her mother Julia's life properly speaking ceased in youth with the sudden death of her idolized first husband, Herbert Duckworth, after only four years of marriage. The traumatized widow would lie down upon his grave as upon a nuptial bed. Her fixed and dedicated grief survived into her second marriage with Virginia's father and found its vocation (which is also Mrs Ramsay's, and the reason for the errand to the lighthouse) in self-sacrificial vigils at sick-beds and the service of afflicted humanity. Photographs of Julia Stephen all show a severe dolour that speaks to a viewer sepulchrally of the absence of that much-painted emblem of the Victorian age, Hope, frequently alluded to in her daughter's writings, with her blindfold eyes and lyre. Julia's eyes were wide open and, irrecoverably, had seen Death:

Never did anybody look so sad. Bitter and black, half-way down, in the darkness, in the shaft which ran from the sunlight to the depths, perhaps a tear formed; a tear fell; the waters swayed this way and that, received it, and were at rest. Never did anybody look so sad. (p. 31)

In *To the Lighthouse*, Beauty is always vitiated thus by sorrow. The self can blacken to a lightless mineshaft, with all the tears it has ever shed collected at the base in corrosive staleness. The refrain 'Never did anybody look so sad' is not only a memorial dirge but a tart comment, judging from tone, which shakes its head at a grief so professional.

To the Lighthouse has its death's head – the pig's skull, nailed to the nursery wall and covered from Cam's panicky view by the green, maternal shawl and her mother's lulling fairy-tale fabrications. In the central section during which Mrs Ramsay dies in parentheses far away, and almost nothing human frequents the house, the shawl gradually loosens and swings free, co-operating with the house's recidivist inclination to collapse into the natural world. The mother's stories have worked to disguise the *memento mori* in a comforting shroud; the daughter-author's story ruthlessly discloses the reality behind the tale-teller's veil, anatomizing as her friend T. S. Eliot did 'the skull beneath the skin'. This is perhaps a bitter comment on the tenuousness of mother-comfort in the mortal, mutable world. *To the Lighthouse* is obsessed by Time as anxiously as Shakespeare's *Sonnets*, which Mrs Ramsay is reading in the final scene of Part One:

> Yet seem'd it winter still, and, you away,
> As with your shadow I with these did play.
>
> (p. 112)

The allusion to Sonnet XCVIII concerns absence and its transformation of an external springtime to an internal winter – abortive, needy loss on a darkening planet. Virginia Woolf has temporarily revived the shadows of her parents and played them in the theatre of her art. This consummating scene, in which the beloved parents sit and read together in deep, still, marital harmony represents the author's lingering valediction and blessing upon them before she consigns them to the maelstrom of the central section, 'Time Passes'. In *To the Lighthouse*, Time blinks away the protective vine-leaf membrane that delicately mantles our childish eye and suffuses the lens with soothing colour like balm. Time takes the players of Part One in a sequence of casual, parenthetical deaths: '[. . . Mrs Ramsay having died rather suddenly the night before . . .]', '[Prue Ramsay died that summer in some illness . . .]', '[. . . Twenty or thirty young men were blown up in France, among them Andrew Ramsay . . .]', (pp. 120, 123, 124). Time disintegrates Mrs Ramsay's perfect moment of peace and wholeness at the dinner-party and unmakes her work of love immediately it is accomplished; it threatens the very materials of Lily's immortalizing art-work, and this act of destruction is, as she realizes, implicit in the very moment of completion: 'It would be hung in the attics, she thought; it would be destroyed. But what did that matter?' (p. 191). *To the Lighthouse* successfully records the failure of art to stem the tides of Time. Some of its unique power and truthfulness resides in the fact that it acknowledges its own frailty, a talent akin to walking on the water, or rooting itself like Mr Ramsay in meditation, as a guidepost out to sea.

Lily, the 'skimpy old maid, holding a paint-brush on the lawn', (p. 167) appears as an artist-persona for the author, a relict who makes new life for herself by memorializing the lost object of desire. Some of the modernity of *To the Lighthouse* belongs to the fact that, like Joyce's *Portrait of the Artist as a Young Man*, the novel takes itself to some degree as its own subject-matter. The difficulty for a woman of attaining self-confidence enough to hold the pen or brush with a calm hand, maintaining the courage and authority of her own vision, is communicated through Lily's struggle for expression. Charles Tansley's 'Women can't write, women can't paint', which saps the power of her ego and wastes her creative energy; Mr Ramsay's sucking at women for sympathy; Mrs Ramsay's determination that 'Lily must marry' and that the single life for a woman is an impairment, all represent a forcefield of internalized pressures against which Lily's modest but genuine gift must self-consumingly struggle for survival. Her virgin spirit is made very beautiful to us as readers. Fierce, self-critical, shy and judicious, she stands like a single child of Artemis amongst the company of Aphrodite. Her plain face and the singularity of her quiet, methodical ways suggest a literary inheritance from *Jane Eyre*, *Villette* and *Agnes Grey* as a woman socially little valued as lacking the passports of beauty, prestige and marriageability, but inscribed with inner human value by her creator.

Whereas Joyce's artist-hero is a writer like himself, Virginia Woolf casts her self-projection as a visual artist, giving a subtle and complex turn to the motif. The novel is a work of words but it functions for us as a sequence of luminous images – each reader will carry away a favourite cluster by which to glean and recall the essence of *To the Lighthouse*. We relate to one another what we feel we have 'seen' in a Virginia Woolf novel, as if recounting dreams. The novel ends on the word 'vision': 'Yes, she thought, laying down her brush in extreme fatigue, I have had my vision' (p. 192). Both the novel and the diary record Virginia Woolf's dissatisfaction with language, in its timebound failure to achieve the illusion of simultaneity (the root of the experimental use of parentheses and the oscillation between perspectives in Part Three) and in the gap between conception and articulation. Writing Part Three, she meditated:

Suppose one could catch them [one's thoughts] before they became 'works of art'? Catch them hot & sudden as they rise in the mind – walking up Asheham hill for instance. Of course one cannot; for the process of language is slow & deluding. One must stop to find a word; then, there is the form of the sentence, soliciting one to fill it. (*Diary*, III, p. 102)

Lily's search for the form of the painting, which occupies her over the whole span of the book, is also 'slow and deluding' but, once achieved, its eternizing fixity outdoes the possibilities of language: the composition of visual images has a holistic suggestiveness which words, simply because they proceed like music in time can emulate but never equal. The triptych structure of *To the Lighthouse* may be interpreted as an attempt to assimilate the imagistic possibilities of language to those of painting, with Lily and her brush a kind of composite figure for Virginia and her sister Vanessa, a Post-Impressionist painter, interested in form and design in art and a flattening monumentality of image, reducing forms to their simplest components as Lily aims to do, and implying the tension between them as a structural principle. Vanessa's *Studland Beach* of 1912–13 exemplifies a technique which we can recognize Virginia appropriating into language in *To the Lighthouse*. Lily refuses an art of verisimilitude (urbanely mocked in the Gallic preciosity of the fashionable landscape painting of the Hebridean scene which Mr Pauncefort inaugurated). Lily paints a mother-and-child as 'a purple shadow'. Her author is 'painting' the identical scene through the eye of Lily, framing the canvas in the binding of a book, reproducing paint by daubing with colourful, shapely words, the pen producing sweeps and blocks of energy on the page through its abstracting illusionism:

But the picture was not of them, she said. Or, not in his sense. There were other senses, too, in which one might reverence them. By a shadow here and a light there, for instance. Her tribute took that form, if, as she vaguely supposed, a picture must be a tribute. A mother and child might be reduced to a shadow without irreverence. (p. 52)

Through reproducing Lily's explanation of her modernist technique, Virginia Woolf is able to make an oblique account of her own literary manner to the reader. If we read *To the Lighthouse* in terms of 'the relations of masses, of lights and shadows' (p. 52), we are well on the way to understanding the implications of Virginia Woolf's abandonment of the conventions of the realistic novel – chapter divisions, omniscient narrator, characterization, exposition, centrality of plot and pre-eminence of dialogue: in fact all those stylizations that lead us to imagine that the persons described might well be performing the actions described in another room and that if only we could find the door we might join and cross-question them. We cannot engage in conversation with a 'purple shadow' nor attribute our own assumptions to 'lights and shadows', any more than we should think of imposing human norms on a problem in physics. It is significant that Lily is explaining her ideas to the scientist, William Bankes: 'He took it scientifically in complete good faith' (p. 52). We are being trained to read language according to a new and demanding code, in which pure consciousness rather than individual personality is mediated through connotative language rather as a purple shadow may realize emotion without direct reference to the unknowable object it declares. Vanessa Bell was herself very drawn to painting the iconography of madonna and child, as Lily is, the ancient male *topos* radically reinvented by the modern woman artist. The attraction to power of colour and tension between forms typifies both sisters. *To the Lighthouse* is a uniquely *painted* book, rich – sometimes lurid – in cardinal colours. Reduced to its palette, one very short paragraph in Part One runs: *soft deep green – greenery – purple passion flowers – high blue – silver wing – red-hot pokers – blue waters – bluer* (p. 23). If we are attentive to what Virginia Woolf calls this 'pulse of colour' throughout the book, we may arrive at the slightly surprising

19

impression of *To the Lighthouse*, in its brilliancy of coloration and extravagance of response to the most minute of visual stimuli, as an incomparably sensual work. In her thin-skinned susceptibility, the author's sensitivity to Beauty – approaching that of Septimus Smith in *Mrs Dalloway* – resembles a Keatsian agony. 'Beauty, the world seemed to say ... To watch a leaf quivering in the rush of air was an exquisite joy' (*Mrs Dalloway*, p. 77). Waves of hallucinatory colour and sentience wash through *To the Lighthouse*, bringing its effects oddly close to that nightmarish extreme of receptiveness which George Eliot figures as the extreme of her doctrine of sympathy: we would hear 'the grass grow and the squirrel's heart beat, and we should die of that roar which lies on the other side of silence' (*Middlemarch*, p. 226). Beauty in Virginia Woolf is seldom tempered to the shorn lamb.

In Joyce but not in Woolf the artist, however ironized, is the artwork's hero. We would not think of subtitling *To the Lighthouse* 'A Portrait of the Artist as a Young Woman'; its dispersed focus forbids any such magnification of the authorial ego. But the spirit of the whole might be coined in a subtitle such as 'A Portrait of Woman as Artist'. The work of creation is here overwhelmingly attributed to woman, in a continuum through Mrs Ramsay, through Lily, to the cleaning lady, Mrs McNab, and her co-worker, Mrs Bast, in the second Part. Mrs Ramsay for a few meaningful moments resolves the vacant, moody, irritable ruminations of her dinner-guests into something resembling a secular sacrament. 'Nothing need be said; nothing could be said. There it was all round them. It partook ... of eternity' (p. 97). The luminous moment that fades into the past even as it reaches consummation is an affirmation of the power of human social love against the flood-tide of darkness that surges against the window-pane outside the candle-lit fellowship at the table. It is in essence the same principle that drives Lily to compose her picture, an art of 'merging and flowing and creating' (p. 79), to pour forth energy so as to reconcile the touchy, nerve-strung and incompatible egos so that 'the walls of partition' (p. 105) between people melt away, and feeling 'is all one stream'. The allusion here is to St Paul's Letter to the Ephesians:

For he is our peace, who hath made both one, and hath broken down the middle wall of partition between us. (2.14)

To the Lighthouse silently rephrases: *She* is our peace. Allowing for Mrs Ramsay's own state of illusion (Paul's and Minta's marriage will be a failure) and her manifold vanities and manipulativeness, the text still transmits this commitment to unity as one of the most precious human art-forms.

At the centre of the novel occurs the desecration of the form that houses such woman-made peace, by Time, nature and the man-made War that decimated Europe. The novel becomes a poem in which the function of the elegy to mourn its dead and query meaning in its totality is conducted in terms of an apocalyptic vision of utmost distress. The centre of *To the Lighthouse* is a *Totentanz* figuring the crematorium of Europe and the evacuation of all that contains, comforts and articulates the human shape, from the walls of a house to the thumb of an empty glove. The narrative voice sardonically sings of the orgy of destruction, collaboratively and jarringly off-key, like moments in Britten's setting of Wilfred Owen's lyrics as *The War Requiem*. The fall of Mrs Ramsay's green shawl from the concealed death's head is likened to the rending asunder of the veil of the Temple at Christ's protracted giving-up of the ghost (p. 124). The rotting house is an echo-chamber for Europe's throes, in which the reverberant thudding of mortars from the continent cracks the teacups and tinkles the glass in the cupboards, as at the shrieking pandemonium of a giant voice. The rape of the home by nature is presented as an event more appalling than the sack of Troy or of Jerusalem. In Virginia Woolf's Post-Christian vision, the household is the only sacred sanctuary known to man and the upkeep of that house the sole priestly function. The ancient competition between the practical life and the life of thought – the *vita activa* and the *vita contemplativa* – forms one of the book's central dichotomies. Lily, Mr Ramsay, Mr Bankes, Charles Tansley and Mr Carmichael profess the *vita contemplativa*, as does the narrative voice itself. Mrs Ramsay, with her managing of the household and her contemplation of the meaning of her world, embraces both. In Part Two, however, the life of thought has no recuperative part to play. It is helpless against the Deluge, a lonely voice like Echo in her cave – or, indeed, worse than useless, a collusive and death-wishing singer of destruction. It considers the over-running of the house by:

... the thistle and the swallow, the rat and the straw. Nothing now withstood them; nothing said no to them. Let the wind blow; let the poppy seed itself and the carnation mate with the cabbage. Let the swallow build in the drawing-room; and the thistle thrust aside the tiles, and the butterfly sun itself on the faded chintz of the armchairs. Let the broken glass and the china lie out on the lawn and be tangled over with grass and wild berries. (pp. 128–9)

The bizarre beauty of the passage, with its ambivalent tone somewhere between rage and resignation, urges on the process of recrudescence with a saturnalian relish at the unmaking of codified meaning. The bastard plant of carnation–cabbage; the penetrating, mouth-filling 'thistle' that 'thrusts'; the butterfly forming a new pattern with the print of the liberated armchair; the strewing of 'glass' in 'grass' with the freeing of all objects from their subservience to human utility imply – in a wonderful spree of *laissez faire* – the wild abdication of the composing narrative voice from any obligation to maintain the human inheritance. But the defeat of the *vita contemplativa* opens the way for the *vita activa*:

Slowly and painfully, with broom and pail, mopping, scouring, Mrs McNab, Mrs Bast stayed the corruption and the rot; rescued from the pool of Time that was fast closing over them now a basin, now a cupboard ... Attended with the creaking of hinges and the screeching of bolts, the slamming and banging of damp-swollen woodwork, some rusty laborious birth seemed to be taking place, as the women, stooping, rising, groaning, singing, slapped and slammed, upstairs now now down in the cellars. Oh, they said, the work! (pp. 129–30)

The holograph manuscript of the novel, which is generally more expository than the finished text, gives a number of clues as to the meaning of the regenerative but mindless figure of Mrs McNab as Virginia Woolf originally conceived her function. She and her helpmeet are comic, uncouth figures, on a curious borderline of characterization where crude caricature meets mythic impersonality, rather like the ancient flower-seller in *Mrs Dalloway* who enjoys a status indeterminate between the human and the animate, being described alternately as an old woman singing and as a rusty pump, 'so rude a mouth, a mere hole in the earth' (p. 91). The manuscript makes clear that it is the very empty-mindedness of the two cleaning women that makes possible the 'rusty laborious birth' of the house from its own corruption. A marginal query reads, 'ask them what the war had been about – did they know?' [sic] (*Holograph Manuscript of To the Lighthouse*, p. 229). The query assimilates the pair to the Romantic *topos* best exemplified by Wordsworth's *Old Cumberland Beggar*, in which a mysterious natural virtue is attributed to a blank mind, and to his *Idiot Boy* which detects a prelapsarian sublimity in the witless or crazed. The lowest of the low intellectually are seen as immune from infection by a society of whose ins and outs they remain profoundly unconscious. To remain in perfect ignorance of the War is to be unimplicated. The restorers of Mrs

Ramsay's house are viewed as a composite power in the universe of the novel which opposes the contrary powers of destruction, just as Mrs Ramsay had composed the self-interested faces round her dinner table into one glow of amity, and just as Lily will fetch out her incomplete picture and set herself to attain unity in its composition. They represent 'a force working; something not highly conscious' (p. 129), a co-operative female endeavour through time to thwart Time. At the conclusion of their labour of renewal, the author signs off their enterprise with the phrase, 'it was finished' (p. 131). So also when Lily Briscoe completes her picture of the house's meaning with one final decisive stroke of her brush, at the end of the novel, the author concludes on her behalf, 'It was done; it was finished' (p. 192). It is one of the lovelier touches in this beautifully wrought novel that the complex, deeply emotional resonance of this phrase should bring to a quietus both the brush-work of the menial and the brush-work of the artist; giving the dignity and pathos of an act of atonement to the creative endeavour of women, for Christ's words on the cross, *Consummatum est*, *It is finished*, complete a ritual of love with the entire surrender of self: 'and he bowed his head, and gave up the ghost' (St John, 19:30). The compositions of art, for Virginia Woolf, are founded on raw loss and pain, and in some sense speak up atoningly for the whole human race. As Lily prepares to lay down the brush, Virginia Woolf prepares to lay aside her pen, so that her *It is finished* consummates the endeavour of all who have fought to create form out of the abyss, resolving the ancient antipathy between the *vita activa* and the *vita contemplativa*.

To the Lighthouse presents a profound concern with gender, and a complex and problematic meditation upon the differences between man and woman. Superficially, the distinction made by the novel between Mr and Mrs Ramsay, and the kinds of thinking they exemplify polarizes gender in a traditional way, but reverses the conventional values society ascribes to the sexes. Mr and Mrs Ramsay stand as archetypal Father and Mother, and are assessed for the qualities of their minds rather as if they were embodied forces of nature or the mythological essence of male and female. They are, like Milton's Adam and Eve, 'our first parents', and divide between them the scale of human possibility. Mrs Ramsay's intuitive, holistic, creative and imaginative mind is opposed and answered by Mr Ramsay's analytic, rationalist and literalistic understanding. They speak two languages, a 'yes' language of woman ('But it may be fine – I expect it will be fine' [p. 10]) and a 'no' language of man ('But it won't be fine' [p. 9, also see pp. 41]), implying opposite ways of viewing truth, Mrs Ramsay interpreting fact by love, and exaggerating her stories, Mr Ramsay respecting plain truth and subjecting it to logical scrutiny. The opposition is set out most powerfully in Section 7 of Part One, in which Mr Ramsay launches his demand for sympathy on his wife. A pattern of symbolic denotations emerges as the dynamic of their relationship, which is easy to evaluate if we set out paradigms of significant phrases against one another:

female
pour erect
a rain of energy
a column of spray
energies . . . fused into force
burning and illuminating
delicious fecundity
fountain and spray of life
circle of life
fertile
flashed her needles
confident, upright
strength flaring up to be drunk
    and quenched
nurse carrying light across a
    dark room
capacity to surround and protect
lavished and spent
rise in a rosy-flowered fruit tree

male
beak of brass (1)
barren and bare
barrenness
want, have, demand
again and again

beak of brass (2)
the arid scimitar of the male
    which smote mercilessly

beak of brass (3)
arid scimitar of his father
plunged and smote

Mr Ramsay's assault on Mrs Ramsay's sympathies is mental and verbal but is presented through symbolism which interprets it as a version of rape. Virginia Woolf chronicles a sequence of remorseless and violent acts of repeated appropriation in as close to a description of the sexual act as her writing ever goes. Seen through the eyes of the competitive boy-child, James, Mr Ramsay's is the behaviour of an oversize infant snatching at the object of desire till, appeased, he desists, 'like a child who drops off satisfied', the predatory, unweanable offspring of the source of life. The almost formulaic character of the passage, with its alliterative patterns and hypnotic insistences, becomes

24

visually impressive in the paradigm of phrases. The symbolism connoting maleness (*beak of brass* with its threefold repetition; *scimitar*) pertains to that which is mechanical and fabricated, having metallic solidity, like a weapon. It is an image of towering menace, sinister in proportion to the ungovernability of its need (*want, have, demand*; *plunged and smote*). However, the symbolism of the female is also, more prolifically, an articulation of power: organic power, all liquidity and emanation. She is the water of life itself, he the greedy drinker. Her ruth is answered by his ruthlessness; that which yields is attacked by that which needs. In this conversation of opposites, creativity is attributed exclusively to the female, in imagery drawn overwhelmingly from 'The Song of Solomon':

A garden inclosed is my sister, my spouse; a spring shut up, a fountain sealed . . .
A fountain of gardens, a well of living waters, and streams from Lebanon. (4: 12, 15)

Mrs Ramsay as a 'rain of energy', a 'column of spray' that 'pour[s] erect', the 'fountain and spray of life' suggests power without destructiveness, nature as an exploited commodity desecrated by that mechanical grotesque, the 'beak of brass barren and bare' with its stabbing automatism of alliteration. Could James the Oedipal child, repeatedly described as standing 'stiff between her legs' in beetle-browed and impotent wrath, conceivably have thought any of this? The narrative voice itself seems to take over completely from him, swelling with its own rage, putting the case against the male and for the female in a festival of denunciation.

Yet to take this confrontation as definitive of the gender-scheme proposed by *To the Lighthouse* would falsify the novel. We know from the essay *A Room of One's Own* (1929) that Virginia Woolf believed in the phenomenon of the 'androgynous mind': 'It is fatal to be a man or woman pure and simple; one must be woman-manly or man-womanly' (p. 99). Such a position has been condemned by modern feminists because it is held to be founded in the traditional stereotypes (woman = emotion, man = intellect), but in practice it has proved a liberating and energizing perspective, allowing for multifarious possibilities in human nature. Although Virginia Woolf does not seem to have been familiar with Jung, her conception approximates closely to that of the Jungian *animus* and *anima*, regarding wholeness and integration as the ideal to which personality strives. Virginia Woolf's source for the idea is Coleridge: 'He meant, perhaps, that the androgynous mind is resonant and porous; that it transmits emotion without impediment; that it is naturally creative, incandescent and undivided' (p. 94). If we measure this statement against the creativity, incandescence and wholeness of being ascribed to Mrs Ramsay in the symbolic paradigm constructed from *To the Lighthouse*, we can see that what is claimed for the 'androgynous' sensibility in *A Room of One's Own* is there claimed for the 'feminine'. This contradiction is sustained if we turn to the second generation of characters in *To the Lighthouse*. The world has moved on from the Victorian gender-distinctions practised and praised in the mother- and father-world. To Mr Ramsay's lexicon of groans and sighs, Lily is deaf and dumb: she has her profession, her cool kind intellect and her autonomy to protect, previously the male prerogative. The androgynous sensibility has come to maturity in Part Three. We might call Lily woman-manly and the adolescent James perhaps man-womanly, in the closeness of his perceptions to the source in his mother. 'One wanted fifty pairs of eyes to see with', reflects Lily, toward the book's conclusion (p. 182); 'nothing was simply one thing', ponders James almost simultaneously. The consensus of their minds on the essential volatility of the world into which they have entered is an index of the commitment of the novel to the incompatibility of its own suggestions, the shifting and variable surface of reality – including the gendering of reality – as if perception were a sliding sea of mesmerizing images like that on which Mr Ramsay's little company is wayfaring to the lighthouse.

The ambivalence, obscurity and multiplicity of truth are central to the manner and method of the novel. Inspecting herself under many *personae*, as artist, as her father's girl, as her mother's child, Virginia Woolf also looks over the reader's shoulder as if to scan his or her reflection in the mirroring text of her novel. An extant photograph of the young Virginia Woolf shows her vigilantly observing her parents as they read. *To the Lighthouse* is full of people reading. Mr Carmichael's entire life seems to be lived in a book; Mrs Ramsay reads to her son the story of The Fisherman and his Wife, 'reading and thinking, quite easily, both at the same time; for the story . . . was like the bass gently accompanying a tune, which now and then ran up unexpectedly into the melody' (p. 55). Snatches of the story accordingly register as part of Virginia Woolf's story, as do Mr Ramsay's fragmentary, fierce renditions of Tennyson's *Charge of the Light Brigade*, his incantation of *Luriana Lurilee* whose hypnotic chant becomes a musical refrain for the novel itself, oddly carrying the burden of Mrs Ramsay's thought though she cannot decipher the words' meaning (p. 102), Shakespeare's *Sonnets*, Cowper's *The Castaway*, Scott's *Waverley* novels. The novel anthologizes this scatter of quotations, acts of reading or remembrances of books once read, less as presenting allusive clues to meaning, as in the practice of earlier novelists, than as part of the flowing mental content of the reading or listening character. As we sit and read our paperback copies of *To the Lighthouse*, we reflect on the characters' interpretation of books we too might reach down from a shelf and share. The novel becomes, symphonically inclusive at such points, like a music in which the audience deliciously participates. The quiet joy of reading is again and again presented to our eye and mind, the joy into which we at the same moment enter, something private but also oddly impersonal, a vast intimate pool of silent thoughtfulness available to all the company of the literate through time. The quoted texts are in solution with the reading character's mind, which in turn is in solution with the novel's narrative voice, which in turn is in solution with the reader's mind at the moment of perception. In an essay of 1913, on Jules Romaine's *Les Copains*, she wrote of this avant garde French writer who had abolished 'characters', humour and plot in his novel, that:

what he delights and excels in doing is to trace the mysterious growth, where two or three are gathered together, of a kind of consciouness of the group in addition to that of each individual of the group. (*The Essays of Virginia Woolf*, Vol. II, p. 17)

Something analagous, though not identical, occurs in the synthesis of inner voices Virginia Woolf makes when she presents the character as reader. The act of reading is figured by *To the Lighthouse* as a loss of self, a balm of relief and release from the painful tic of self-consciousness which afflicts most of Virginia Woolf's persons. One goes down into a book to submerge, rest and replenish the self, as if to sleep and dream. In a novelistic world where sexuality is feared and sleep hard-come-by, the joy of books appears almost as sensual surrender.

The consummation of Part One, our last vision of the parents together, is a conclusive celebration of their underlying marital unity. The static rendering of the iconography of the Parents reading in their chairs has the iconic feel of a Henry Moore sculpting of the essential relations of the Father and Mother as the supportive pillars of the universe, the source and terminus of all being. We respond especially to the quietness and repose of the two figures in relation to one another, the subsiding of irritability and desire into the sharing of an unselfconscious, unworried rootedness, suggested in the image of a tree whose 'tossing and quivering' leaves settle 'leaf by leaf, into quiet' (p. 109). The harmonious balance they hold in relation to one another is the perfection of the *vita contemplativa* in mutual but separate recesses of the spirit. This father–mother icon mirrors and balances the mother–son composition which opens the book and is displaced by the father's interruption; now Mrs Ramsay wants to interrupt her husband to share his privacy:

he did not want to be interrupted – that was clear. He was reading something that moved him very much. He was half smiling and then she knew he was controlling his emotion. He was tossing the pages over. He was acting it – perhaps he was thinking himself the person in the book. She wondered what book it was. Oh, it was one of old Sir Walter's, she saw . . . (p. 108)

There are so many ways of reading a book. Mr Ramsay's is an energetic procedure, involving passionate behaviour in regard to turning pages, the twitching of lips, the slapping of thighs (pp. 109–10). Mrs Ramsay's is quiet and lulled: 'She looked very peaceful, reading' (p. 111). As we read the two of them reading, and scanning one another's countenances and gestures to 'read' for responses and interpretations, we embrace their privacy in our own deep mimesis of their act. We are 'deep' in the book like them, and the 'words, like little shaded lights' which 'lit up in the dark of her mind' (p. 109) are opened out to our inspection. In a world of multiply discrepant eye-lines, to share this peace of reading is to meet along a line of vision. When we share a room with someone absorbed in a book, primal curiosity is aroused: 'She wondered what book it was'. The reader inhabits a secret world, and lies open to observation in a very vulnerable way, like a sleeper by a wakeful voyeur.

Reading in *To the Lighthouse* is assimilated to the experience of sleep. Mrs Ramsay resembles someone 'in a light sleep' who is reluctant to wake, 'but otherwise, might she go on sleeping, just a little longer . . .?' (p. 111). The association of reading with 'being asleep in broad daylight' (p. 112) carries an emotional weight strangely similar to the Haidée episode in Byron's *Don Juan*:

> For there it lies so tranquil, so beloved,
>   All that it hath of life with us is living;
> So gentle, stirless, helpless, and unmoved,

> And all unconscious of the joy 'tis giving;
> All it hath felt, inflicted, pass'd, and proved,
>   Hush'd into depths beyond the watcher's diving;
> There lies the thing we love with all its errors
> And all its charms, like death without its terrors.
> (Canto II. CXCVII)

The vulnerable openness of the sleeper to the waker, his submergence in an inscrutable sea of unconsciousness and the likeness of the spirit's retirement to 'death without its terrors' are emotionally close to the suggestiveness of Virginia Woolf's tender account of her parents' mutual reverie. For the watcher, there is an almost illicit pondering of a person whose defences are surrendered; for the 'sleeping' reader, there is a wish not to resume the life of consciousness. The shadow of death falls across the conclusion of Part 1 ('the shadow, the thing folding them in was beginning, she felt, to close round her again' [p. 113]), and all remains flawed and inconclusive – Minta's problematic marriage; Mr Ramsay's secret contempt for his wife's intelligence; her acknowledgement that she won't finish in time the stocking which she's been fussing over throughout; her confession that they will not go to the lighthouse, conceding her husband's case, in her last utterance of the whole novel, reversing her first words. Yet what we carry away with us is a tableau of married love realized by books' catharsis of people's best emotion: Mr Ramsay raising his book to hide the tears it draws (p. 110); his fellowship with his reading wife – 'Go on reading. You don't look sad now, he thought' (p. 112).

Virginia Woolf's high valuation of books as the essence of civilization and the immortalization of our highest hopes is deep in the humanist tradition. '(A)s well almost kill a Man as kill a good Book,' wrote Milton in *Areopagitica*, his defence of freedom of the press.

For Books are not absolutely dead things, but doe contain a potencie of life in them to be as active as that soule was whose progeny they are; nay they do preserve as in a violl the purest efficacie and extraction of that living intellect that bred them. (*Areopagitica*, p. 492)

We need to remember that the author of *To the Lighthouse* was a publisher and printer, the co-founder of the Hogarth Press, as well as an author. 'I'm the only woman in England free to write what I like,' she remarked in the Diary (Vol. III, p. 43) early in the writing of the novel, meaning that the medium of production was in her own hands; she could be subjected to no censorship. Both her essays and *To the*

Lighthouse itself testify to her pleasure and fascination in the feel of the book in her hands, the quality of its paper and binding, the world-containing object. Fulminating against *Lord Jim*'s 'sad green colour . . . sprinkled with chocolate-brown nautical emblems', weighing 'a slim little book in our hands', greeting 'another red volume' of Dostoevsky (*The Essays of Virginia Woolf*, Vol. II, pp. 140, 73, 83), she constantly reminds the readers of her prolific reviews that the book is a whole unit, body and soul, matter and spirit. Hence, it, like the man who weighs it in his hands, is capable of death. Part Two of *To the Lighthouse* witnesses the barbarous destruction not only of the youth of Europe but also, along with the desecration of the mother's hearth, the devastation of literature itself, the lamp of civilization. As a chorus of voices greets the torrential darkness closing in during the first Section of Part Two ('"It's almost too dark to see"; "Andrew . . . just put out the light in the hall"' p. 117), there is an unmistakable allusion to Virginia Woolf's Augustan heritage:

> She comes! she comes! the sable Throne behold
> Of *Night* Primaeval, and of *Chaos* old! . . .
>
> As one by one, at dread Medea's strain,
> The sick'ning stars fade off th'ethereal plain;
> As Argus' eyes by Hermes' wand opprest,
> Clos'd one by one to everlasting rest;
> Thus at her felt approach, and secret might,
> *Art* after *Art* goes out, and all is Night.
> See skulking *Truth* to her old Cavern fled,
> Mountains of Casuistry heap'd o'er her head!
> *Philosophy*, that lean'd on Heav'n before,
> Shrinks to her second cause, and is no more . . .
>
> Lo! thy dread Empire, CHAOS! is restor'd;
> Light dies before thy uncreating word:
> Thy hand, great Anarch! lets the curtain fall;
> And Universal Darkness buries all.
> (Pope, *Dunciad*, IV. 629–30, 635–44, 653–6)

One by one the lamps were all extinguished, except that Mr Carmichael, who liked to lie awake a little reading Virgil, kept his candle burning rather longer than the rest.

2

So with the lamps all put out, the moon sunk, and a thin rain drumming on the roof a downpouring of immense darkness began . . . [Here Mr Carmichael, who was reading Virgil, blew out his candle. It was past midnight.] (pp. 117–18)

This is the last act of reading to be recorded in the ten-year central Part in which the Great Anarch of the modern world – Europe's male politicians, the underworld of the mortal planet – enacts another death of humanism to equal or outdo that with which Pope's *Dunciad* had contended. In the tenth Section, Mr Carmichael resumes his reading by candle-light (p. 132), having been the only character in the novel to have profited by the War, in his successful volume of poetry (p. 125). As the reader of Virgil, he is maintaining an ancient, classical legacy of light into the present day, preserving Milton's 'potencie of life' in the vial of the book, illuminating his mind with the testament of civilization. But he too must 'blow out his candle' and sleep.

Scott's *Waverley* novels trace a passage through each Part of *To the Lighthouse* – Mr Ramsay's favourites, all vigour, humour and humanity, housing their immortal stories in perishable covers. In Part Two they moulder on the shelves ('All those books needed to be laid out on the grass in the sun' [p. 126]) and are 'fetched up from oblivion' in company with a teaset one morning (p. 129) just in time to escape complete dereliction. In Part Three they have been restored to Mr Ramsay's hands, and Cam contemplates him in the boat 'reading the little book with the shiny cover mottled like a plover's egg' (p. 175). Cam feels safe with the old gentleman reading; her thoughts now are an unspoken benediction, and her perception of the patterning on the old book as resembling a plover's egg associates the book with fertility and spring. For the reader there is a sensation of relief at the salvage of 'the little book with yellowish pages' which Virginia Woolf memorializes, perhaps from her own father's collection:

It was small; it was closely printed; on the fly-leaf, she knew, he had written that he had spent fifteen francs on dinner; the wine had been so much; he had given so much to the waiter; all was added up neatly at the bottom of the page. But what might be written in the book which had rounded its edges off in his pocket, she did not know. What he thought they none of them knew. But he was absorbed in it . . . (p. 176)

If each person in *To the Lighthouse* may be imagined as a lighthouse, illumining the world with a singular eye-beam, of a certain luminosity, from an individual perspective, so also each may be conceived as a living book. These human books are filled with memos, lists, marginalia, all the fascinating random trivia of a life, in the handwriting that spells one as *this* person and no other. Cam is touched and curious at her father's jottings in the old book which so absorbs him. The old book is as inscrutable and imperfectly legible as he himself is to her ('she did not know') and as all character is felt to be in *To the Lighthouse* ('they none of them knew'). At the hieroglyphic writing of the occult human spirit – 'tablets bearing sacred inscriptions' (p. 50) – the narrative voice marvels, guesses, improvises, conjectures, but finally claims to know nothing more than that it cannot know.

The literary equivalent of multiple perspectivism in visual art predominates in *To the Lighthouse*, which is committed to measure and ratio as it tirelessly plots the line of vision between perceiver and perceived. If we imagine a play of many searchlights sweeping in countless permutations in relation to one another, each seeking clarification of the state of darkness here below, we may come near to producing a mental image of the breath-taking complexity – always shifting and realigning – with which the author angles the lines of vision in the novel. As a character moves around the compass of his world, so the play of his searchlight changes; and of course all the other characters move round fractionally in discrepant ways in relation to him. Hence a reader eager to grasp every detail of meaning may often feel the urge to reach for a pencil and chart the whereabouts of each character in the garden in Part One, for a slight change of direction taken by the legs (Mr Ramsay's trajectory, for instance) may often signal a complete *peripeteia* of the mind's vision. Hence in Section 8, Mrs Ramsay and James remain the static objects of perception at the window; Mr Carmichael cryptically shuffles past, wincing away from her (pp. 41–3) and precipitating her into a moment of self-distrust; Mr Ramsay stops, nods, turns away on his peripatetic journey round the garden, moves to the edge of the lawn, stops and looks out to sea. Here, his whole mental horizon changes, and he loses himself in thought (pp. 44–5). He turns, looks back again to his wife and son (another *peripeteia*); Lily looks at him from her static position at the easel and assesses him at that distance (pp. 45–6); he bears down on her and Mr Bankes; turns again to the sea; turns away again (p. 46). This apparently haphazard and commonplace sequence of movements is documented with the most scholastic care and precision, as if a verbal mathematician plotted a graph intended to be accurate to a hair's-breadth. Associated with this cartography both of the outer and the inner life is the concept (or rather, image) of eye-beams, incorporated into Virginia Woolf's system rather as if they had the scientific status attributed to them by the ancient theory of optics which held sway until the Renaissance and is immortalized poetically in Donne's *Exstasie*: 'Our eye-beams twisted, and did thred/Our eyes, upon one double string' (7–8). In Section 9, Mr Bankes and Lily look with '"rapture", this silent stare' (p. 48) at Mrs Ramsay in the window:

Looking along the level of Mr Bankes's glance at her, she thought that no woman could worship another woman in the way he worshipped; they could only seek shelter under the shade which Mr Bankes extended over them both. Looking along his beam she added to it her different ray, thinking that she was unquestionably the loveliest of people (bowed over her book); the best perhaps; but also, different too from the perfect shape which one saw there. But why different, and how different? she asked herself . . . (pp. 48–9)

The mind confers the light of perception upon externals; does not receive them passively. William Bankes gives out his perceptions along a certain perspective which Lily, standing alongside, seeks to share, to grasp how things look from where he stands, in his maleness and elderliness. From either viewpoint, the reality of the object of perception remains in question. 'But why different, and how different?': rhetorical questions in clusters throughout the novel confess the failure of the individual eye-beam, even in relation to the subtle light of the authorial scanning of the whole, to compose a final and definitive image.

Many of the novel's most beautiful and suggestive effects come from a kind of serious teasing of vision, with a *trompe-l'oeuil* effect. Nancy in Section 14 broods like Omniscience above a rock-pool, magnifying its minnows in imagination into sharks and whales, eclipsing their sunlight with her godlike hand. With her magnifying-glass eye and weather-changing potency, Nancy's play mimes God's callous indifference to the mortal world and exhibits all the tricks of Virginia Woolf's perspectivism in a truly baroque bending of perception:

And then, letting her eyes slide imperceptibly above the pool and rest on that wavering line of sea and sky, on the tree trunks which the smoke of steamers made waver upon the horizon, she became . . . hypnotized . . . (p. 72)

Sliding eyes that measure simultaneously 'two senses of that vastness and this tininess', the ocean and the rock-pool, conjure 'tree trunks' from the sea in smoke from funnels of ships. The illusionism is so masterly that we see the tree rather than the smoke; 'some fantastic leviathan' stalks the sand, and the humble crab is not named. The prose, like bent light in water, refracts the view that meets each character's eye-line. The reader feels he shares the reflection on the lens of the marvelling, awed, world-creating girl. And a change of light is a change of vision. The lighting of the eight candles around the Ramsay table refashions the parameters of vision, transfiguring the dish of fruits at the centre into a mythic world 'of great size and depth ... a world in which one could take one's staff and climb up hills ... and go down into valleys' (p. 90). Mr Carmichael is said to 'feast his eyes' on the same vista. Eyes in *To the Lighthouse* can hunger for, relish and eat into the mind the field of perception, so intense are the novel's visual stimuli. 'That was his way of looking, different from hers. But looking together united them' (p. 90).

In Part Three, the narrative takes a series of bearings on the progress of the Ramsays' boat journeying out to the lighthouse, and further bearings from the boat to the receding shore, as though the narrative trained a theodolite upon its objects of perception, and back again. Whereas the earlier effects of telescopic magnification and microscopic vision owe a general debt to the post-Swiftian tradition which rests on the axiom that 'nothing is great or little otherwise than by comparison' (*Gulliver's Travels*, p. 70), the complex adjustments of optical perspective which structure Part Three construe reality in a way which cannot be imagined as pre-dating the age of Relativity and quantum physics. Lily watches 'the boat take its way with deliberation past the other boats out to sea' (p. 151). Cam in the next Section looks back to the island from the boat and sees an image of peace and freedom: 'They have no suffering there, she thought' (p. 158). We turn again and are with Lily in close-up, anguishing upon the shore, painting 'the problem of space' (p. 159), recalling Mrs Ramsay with such grief that she calls her name: 'The tears ran down her face' (p. 167). Next time she looks out to sea, the boat has reached the half-way mark, and Cam, looking back to the invisible, inaudible Lily, is still sure that 'They don't feel a thing there' (p. 169). By the ninth Section, there is nothing more for Lily to see but distance and calm absence (p. 174), and for Cam only something 'very small; shaped something like a leaf stood on end' (p. 174), then a vanishing blur. Distance, Lily feels, 'elongates' her emotion for Mr Ramsay (p. 177). In this long-drawn-out two-way valediction, we assess the reciprocal eye-lines and deductions from the ironic vantage-point of our double-vision. As Lily's picture resolves itself into a system of triangles, so the complex of divergent measurements made by the novel's characters may suggest to a reader a system of triangular surveys, reading reality upon a multiplicity of axes, with distance, light and angle of vision determining the definition of what is revealed. For all its passionate lyricism, the novel viewed in this light appears as a literary pure mathematics of surpassing obliquity and fanatical meticulousness devoted to the fullest possible exposition and experimental solution of the problems it addresses.

2. A Modernist Prose

How to write a novel? What to write about? How to read it? These questions had all been decided by the law of precedent long ago when Virginia Woolf picked up the pen to undertake her first work of fiction, *The Voyage Out*, in 1909. Her friend E. M. Forster sums up the traditional compact between a writer, his material and manner, and a reader, in the essay 'What Is A Novel?' With rueful irony he defends his own conservatism, or conservationism, as he points out that a novel must, unfortunately, be so simple-minded as to tell a story. It is expected to concern people not unlike ourselves in a realistically observed world. Its plot should observe the Aristotelian proprieties of development from beginning, to middle, to end. Forster's practice demonstrates that he welcomed and did not query the structural conventions of novel-writing, which, for instance, divides the form into self-limiting blocks of plot in chronologically arranged chapters, and supervises the action with an omniscient narrator. 'The poet is twitched away by the satirist; the comedian is tapped on the shoulder by the moralist,' Virginia Woolf objected in her essay on Forster (*The Common Reader*, Vol. I, p. 349), subliminally justifying her own practice rather than doing justice to her friend's. And yet in another essay, 'Mr Bennett and Mrs Brown' of 1924, she includes Forster with the élite of the 'Georgians' (moderns like 'Mr Forster and Mr Lawrence . . . Mr Joyce and Mr Eliot' [pp. 333–4]) as against played-out conventionalists like Arnold Bennett and H. G. Wells. Like Virginia Woolf, Forster questions language itself, both as a viable medium of communication between persons, classes and races and in view of the disintegration of a European consensus faith in a hierarchy of meaning and value in the universe. *A Passage to India* was completed as Virginia Woolf was writing *To the Lighthouse*: the unhinging 'Boum' of the Marabar caves which echoes to make all articulations 'devoid of distinction' (p. 145) and murmurs '"Everything exists, nothing has value"' (p. 147) records the same semantic doubts as animate Virginia Woolf's concern with the broken marriage between words and the reality they denote in *To the Lighthouse*.

In Virginia Woolf's fiction, the breakdown, or breaking open, of traditional literary forms in the light of the twentieth century querying of perception, reality and linguistic meaning, is recorded as a reconceiving of the novel-form in its totality. The old complicity of assumption between author and reader is rejected, in a sequence of experimental fictions, from the innovatory story, *Kew Gardens* (1917), in which Katherine Mansfield saw 'a still quivering changing light over it all and a sense of those couples dissolving in the bright air which fascinates me' (*Letter to VW*, August, 1917). This challenge to official ways of measuring proportion, light, time and human character develops through *Jacob's Room* (1922), *Mrs Dalloway* (1925), *To the Lighthouse* (1927) and culminates in *The Waves* (1931). In some ways, of course, this revolution had been implicit in the very tradition it rejected: with hindsight, we can see the novel waiting for Virginia Woolf to dissolve and recreate it. George Eliot, who herself revolutionized the concept of Time in fiction by challenging the whole notion of beginnings and endings in *Daniel Deronda* (1874–6), had written of the novel that, being so young in the family of genres, it lacked the fixity of more antique forms. 'Like crystalline masses, [the novel] may take any form, and yet be beautiful' ('Silly Novels by Lady Novelists', *The Essays of George Eliot*, p. 324). When Virginia Woolf reinvented the novel, she was extending the boundaries of beauty in a manner which is in keeping with the fluid notion George Eliot proposes. Abolishing chapter and verse, Virginia Woolf creates a rhythmic, wave-like form of undulating passages as in music, where the structure of parts within an individual movement is a continuous flow rather than a series of stops and starts. She identifies language itself as a volatile and indeterminate system of mirroring suggestions; reality as potentially unknowable, and the novel form itself as susceptible of radical transformation to accommodate these perspectives.

Virginia Woolf renounces the narrative persona as a sort of privileged extra character testifying to indubitable mental and physical events and evaluating their significance. She shifts significance to the act of mediation itself as a primary subject to be investigated. The focus is on perception itself, the field of consciousness in flux, abstaining from selection between trivial or intense states of consciousness. In *Jacob's Room*, experimentalism dramatizes the unknowability of an individual self by writing all around his contour, filling the room he inhabits but not the space that is Jacob, who remains an inscrutable gap against which other people's desires and assumptions, together with his biographer's speculations, brush inquisitively and fall away. This failure of mutual knowledge is dramatized in *Mrs Dalloway* as a representation of closed interiorities holding incommunicado conversations, interrupted by the chiming of the mortal clock (the novel was provisionally entitled *The Hours*) and mapped as a series of solitary peregrinations round the Westminster area of London. *To the Lighthouse* develops this principle of passing the baton of interior monologue from one character to another by its eavesdropping of the self-sealed consciousness of a group enwrapped in meditation through the round of two life-encapsulating days. The novel charts the flow and recoil of sympathy, the fluctuations of the mind in process of action and reaction, trapped in the idiolect which enshrines the self's mental habits and assumptions, and venturing out in snatches of conversastion and flickers of insight to fellows stranded in the same familial intimacy and alienation. The central section, in which the evacuated house deteriorates, experiments with a covering of language for the absence of all human intercourse; a narrative voice keeps vigil like the eye of the impersonal lighthouse. The Diary records the ease with which she wrote this section:

I cannot make it out – here is the most difficult abstract piece of writing – I have to give an empty house, no people's characters, the passage of time, all eyeless & featureless with nothing to cling to: well, I rush at it, & at once scatter out two pages. Is it nonsense, is it brilliance? Why am I so flown with words, & apparently free to do exactly what I like? (*Diary*, III, p. 76)

Eyeless and featureless: we awaken from our nightmares sweating, and wishing to forget. Virginia Woolf preserves the nightmare and runs it on like a film into the reluctant eye of day. The central section is a testament to reality dehumanized: what is left when the human eye is subtracted from the sum of things; matter drained of spirit, pure as a chair or table or flower viewed by some Teutonic artist prescient of War and death-camps. This keeping of an eye on eyeless nature has affinities with the techniques of surrealism. It deranges perception of the commonplace objects which are our natural surroundings by applying a kind of syringe which sucks out all the consolation of their familiarity, utility and long-standing givenness. Violets and daffodils are customary emblems of pastoral rebirth: each year they are new, but familiar and expected. But the flowers that the all-seeing witness plants in her central Part 'stand( ) there, looking before them, looking up, yet beholding nothing, eyeless, and thus terrible' (p. 125–6). This short Section 7 of Part Two is committed to the madness of the universe in the wake of the foregoing events – deaths, the Great War. Inner chaos is projected upon the universe in a return to Plato's war of the elements, the primal Chaos (*Timaeus*, 52–3). The winds and waves roll round tumultuously like 'leviathans whose brows are pierced by no light of reason, and mounted one on top of one another ... in idiot games' (p. 125). After 'mounted', the manuscript has 'mounting in lust or conquest'. The author's deepest fears are realized in this section in a tumult of eyeless sexuality and violence expressed in the bestial waters rising upon one another and falling into one another, over-running the safe threshold of self. The aura of the strange and sinister is cast on both stillness and motion, in a psychotic terror of ordinary objects, a sick dream of a world instinct with unspecifiable threat, like Sartre's *Nausea*. The flower-heads stand and 'look up' as the English language fancifully and cosily assures us. Like us they have 'heads', and some have 'eyes' like daisies ('day's eye' originally) and pansies ('Pan's eye'). Virginia Woolf's application of language's self-solacing nursery clichés to the actual object admonishes our floral whimsies. Her flower-heads are blind cyclops staring from a blank ball of raw matter. This insanity is the product of taking language as a guide to reality, and the quality of terror communicated to the reader by the prose stems from its imperative on us to recognize that the images in words express *our* needs, systems and impressions and have nothing to do with the world 'out there'. The experimental narrator has entered the empty house through a crack or keyhole like the noxious airs that demolish the house, and borne unobserved and unobservable witness to what lies beyond the rationale of human presence. Strictly speaking, there is nothing to tell. '*Time Passes*', like Donne's *Nocturnall Upon St Lucies Day*, or Rochester's *Ode to Nothing*, Shakespeare's *King Lear* or Beckett's *Waiting For Godot*, trespasses with words in a realm of which nothing can be said:

> ... I am every dead thing,
> In whom love wrought new Alchimie.
> > For his art did expresse
> A quintessence even from nothingnesse,
> From dull privations and lean emptinesse:
> He ruin'd me, and I am re-begot
> Of absence, darknesse, death; things which are not.
> > (Donne, *Nocturnall*, 12–18)

Virginia Woolf described herself as 'flown with words', 'free' to 'scatter out' this difficult, abstract piece of writing: it is one of the major mysteries not only of her art but of literature as a whole that experiences of such appalling pain as this central Part articulates (in this case the recapitulation of her delirium of mental anguish in the wake of her mother's and half-sister's, then her brother's, deaths) can be emptied on to the page as art in such a spirit of intoxicated creativity.

The final Part of *To the Lighthouse* is experimental in a less flamboyant way than the central panel. It experiments with posthumous representation, recording the experience of the absence and reconstruction of the persons whose consciousness dominated the first part of the novel. More exactly – typifying the refinement of the mental processes which inform the novel's technical virtuosity – the final Part reconstructs a reconstruction. Lily's picture and the difficulties of its composition are both subject-matter and a mirror in which Virginia Woolf may study, criticize and perfect her own search for the form of emotional truth, 'how to connect this mass on the right hand with this on the left' (p. 53), or, in literary terms, Part One with Part Three. Through the inset artwork, she enables herself to ponder her own self-consciousness, to anatomize the act of anatomizing, taking fictional thought to an unprecedented level of refinement, a movement toward the purely intellective such as Aristotle intimates when he calls his God's thinking a 'thinking of thinking' (*Metaphysics*, Λ. ix). In this way, Virginia Woolf transforms the excoriated self-consciousness that was such a bane in her personal life, so that to look in a mirror or to appear in new clothes was agony, into a formidable instrument of self-scrutiny. The Diaries confirm that she spent considerable time listening to herself thinking, researching how the words for observations and emotions rose and formed in her mind, together with the nerve-quick motions of adjustment and revision made by the judgment in ordering this initial verbal material. This was no act of narcissism but a long-term controlled experiment in the sources of creativity, the object of study consisting not in a unique mind so much as a representative instance of how the mind operates under specific conditions. Daughter of high-minded Victorian philosophy in this as in other respects, she spied on herself in the interests less of vanity than of truth. As dedicated to the life of thought as Mr Ramsay when he stood 'as a stake driven into the bed of a channel . . . marking the channel out there in the floods alone' (p. 45), the authorial persona of *To the Lighthouse* mediates its persons as solitaries in a voice that has known the extreme of human loneliness and used it as the testing ground of art.

In *To the Lighthouse*, echoing this universal condition of loneliness, the proportion of direct speech to indirect speech is miniscule, and, indeed, rudimentary. If we reduce the first Section of the novel to its dialogue, the following structure emerges:

'Yes, of course, if it's fine to-morrow,' said Mrs Ramsay. 'But you'll have to be up with the lark' . . .
   'But,' said his father . . . 'it won't be fine.'
   'But it may be fine – I expect it will be fine,' said Mrs Ramsay . . .
   'It's due west,' said the atheist Tansley . . .
   'Nonsense,' said Mrs Ramsay . . .
   'There'll be no landing at the Lighthouse to-morrow,' said Charles Tansley . . .
   'Would it bore you to come with me, Mr Tansley?'
   'Let us all go!' she cried . . .
   'Let's go,' he said.
   'Good-bye, Elsie,' she said. (pp. 9–18)

Inconsequent voices demur about the weather: typical English conversation implying a tepid form of phatic communion, signifying little – so we might assess this dialogue if it were presented to us as I have transcribed it, dissecting it from its root-network in the complex matrix of the narrative voice which recounts the interior-soliloquies of the persons from whom these wisps of talk are gathered. The dominant mode of *To the Lighthouse* is multiple impersonation of soliloquies. Indeed, the contribution of the boy James in this first Section, though fierce and uproarious (he would like to murder his father for saying no to the lighthouse) is wholly soliloquy, suppressed into indirect narrative as a child's impulses seethe unvented beneath the pressure of adult omnipotence. It is the narrator's painstaking saying of the unsaid, disclosing the continuum of thoughts which motivate, slant and raise to the power of urgency the tenor of what is said, that infuses the trivial conversation with a quality of tense emergency.

In earlier authors, of course, we find versions of interior monologue, together with (say, in *Middlemarch*) disproportion between dialogue and interpretative comment. But in that the narrator is always potentially distinct from the characters she temporarily inhabits, George Eliot does not approach Virginia Woolf's revolutionary diffusion of narrative self into the inwardness of her characters. The intensity of her focus on the underworld of thought beneath our blandest utterances raises such remarks as are made to archetypal status. 'I dig out beautiful caves behind my characters,' she wrote whilst composing *Mrs Dalloway*, in 1923 (*Diary*, II, p. 263). When Mrs Ramsay speaks encouragingly and Mr Ramsay discouragingly about the trip to the lighthouse, the tension between the father-law and mother-love strings the nondescript lines tight as wire. We feel in this brief exchange about the weather that each is a barometer of weather in antipathetic worlds. The voices, in the context of the underlying soliloquy which is the book's dominant mode, seem choric, especially on our second or third reading of *To the Lighthouse* when we have some idea of the burden of emotion and significance these prosaic words carry. In Mr Ramsay's 'But', detached from the rest of his remark ('it won't be fine') by the grammatical form of the sentence, lies all the crushing weight of paternal reason that ever went over a boy's unshod foot like the wheel of a wagon in his mother's garden (see p. 171); in his mother's optimistic prevarication ('But it may be fine – I expect it will be fine') is the mediatorial sympathy that filmed the childish eye with a protective membrane like 'a very thin yellow veil . . . like a vine leaf' (p. 171) until the optic nerve could tolerate broad daylight. The subchorus of 'the atheist Tansley' reinforces the paternal chant and is in turn, with asperity, countered by the mother's affirmation. The conversation then modulates from dispute to reconciliation; the slammed doors of the spirit open and there is mutual welcome between male and female as Mrs Ramsay and Charles Tansley share their outing ('"come with me", "Let us all go!"') until, with the second Section, the movement of recoil cyclically begins again: '"No going to the Lighthouse, James"' (p. 19). The strandedness of all dialogue within the text, where background strains forward between all utterances and strives to become foreground, like a foreshortened vista between houses, makes all speech in *To the Lighthouse* curiously anonymous, impersonal and free. Comparison with almost any earlier novel reinforces our sense of the apostrophizing nature of Virginia Woolf's dialogue, as if it escaped from her characters like rhetorical questions, unsolicitous of reply. Here are Mr and Mrs Tulliver in George Eliot's *The Mill on the Floss* (1860) discussing the foibles, lovable or irritating, of their intransigent daughter:

'You talk o' 'cuteness, Mr Tulliver,' she observed as she sat down, 'but I'm sure the child's half an idiot i' some things . . . it seems hard as I should have but one gell, an' her so comical.'

'Pooh, nonsense!' said Mr Tulliver, 'she's a straight black-eyed wench as any body need wish to see. I don't know i' what she's behind other folks's children; and she can read almost as well as the parson.'

'But her hair won't curl all I can do with it, and she's so franzy about having it put i' paper, and I've such work as never was to make her stand and have it pinched with th'irons.'

'Cut it off – cut it off short,' said the father rashly. (*The Mill on the Floss*, Ch. 2)

This conversation, in which the father displays a permissive, the mother a repressive attitude, obeys – as Virginia Woolf's dialogue frequently declines to do – all those laws without which interchange in the real world must come to a standstill. The parents' dispute respects the clock that keeps time in the real world outside an artwork, occupying a scarcely longer period of time than it would take to deliver the speeches, stage directions being kept to a minimum and interpretative comment negligible, confining itself to a bubble of irony in the adverb 'rashly'. As we read, we can persuade ourselves without difficulty to hear these voices and apprehend these presences as though they might emanate as apparitions in the room we occupy. In Virginia Woolf, characters are built of thought; their presences are not known as fleshly and they seem to speak in our mind's ear, in solution with our own mental processes.

Utterances in *To the Lighthouse* seem to float in mid-air and are seldom directly answered, with the effect that they become charged with extra-personal significance, like a scattered and fragmentary Greek chorus. The narrative voice becomes a primary agent of interruption, forcing individual participations in conversation apart by obtruding the rich flow of thought-content which motivates, explains, undermines or contradicts what is said. Speech is made to seem a kind of digression from the major business of life: a radical reversal of a traditional emphasis of the novel, where meaning is assumed to be generated by social or personal exchange. In Virginia Woolf, dialogue takes on a ritualistic and static quality. Speech may go unanswered, and indeed the speaker may not appear to be listening out for an answer at all, abandoning interest in communication as likely to prove abortive, to be re-engrossed in the interior world and its endless to and fro, and if and but, of discourse. Questions may be left in mid-air, as at the end of Part One, Section 13, where Mrs Ramsay's question, '"Did Nancy go with them?"' remains unanswered until Section 15, which consists solely of Prue's words, '"Yes ... I think Nancy did go with them"' (pp. 70, 75). Meanwhile, a parenthetical chapter (parentheses being a punctuating signal for simultaneity) transfers the reader to the shore-line and pre-empts for him Prue's reply by an exposition of what Nancy, Andrew, Minta and Paul did there. When the reader reaches Prue's reply, both the questioner and the question have probably been forgotten, and the slightly vertiginous reader leafs back a couple of pages to stabilize himself in the narrative. Narrative time thus betrays the chronology of realistic probability by forcing a gulf between question and answer. Like T. S. Eliot's solipsists in the earlier poems, Virginia Woolf's people speak into silence from wordy consciousnesses which drown out whatever communications might be registered from the outside world. Narrative time is made to stretch between the moments it connects (the measuring of a stocking against a child's leg 'a moment before' he is kissed on the head and forgiven for his fidgeting [pp. 31–2]) aggregating thought-content into a mass of paragraphs whose expansion levers the two events forcefully apart. Two pages of the text we read cover this 'moment'; it will take us several minutes (and Virginia Woolf is slow, intense reading at the best of times) to complete the sequence of actions with the characters. It is as if there were two kinds of time presented in the book: the ponderous blinking of an eye in the external world which is measured by whirling clock-hands in the internal world.

Equivocation between outer and inner events is also a reflex of Virginia Woolf's fictional manner in *To the Lighthouse*. Indeed, the technique makes possible an insecurity in the reader as to whether an external conversation has actually taken place, or simply an internal passage of thought. Characters habitually dispute issues with themselves, or conduct arguments they would like to have with others, in rehearsal. Punctuation is called into play as a revolutionary destabilizer of the status of what is said. Thought fades into speech as though the two were not perceived as distinct. To blur the honourable distinctions between *she thought*, *she said* and *she did* is to place a giant question mark over the whole field of novelistic perception. Arguing through in Part One, Section 6 the same old issue of visiting the lighthouse, Mr and Mrs Ramsay's speech is not mapped by the conventional signals of punctuation:

There wasn't the slightest possible chance that they could go to the Lighthouse to-morrow, Mr Ramsay snapped out irascibly.

How did he know? she asked. The wind often changed. (pp. 33–4)

The status of the utterances here is indeterminate between direct speech and reported speech, and indeed implies a blurring of modes. Absence of quotation marks and use of the past tense indicate reported speech; but the form in which the conversation is laid out on the page suggests the immediacy of direct speech. It is only in the next paragraph when

Mr Ramsay comes out with the oath 'Damn you' that the prose registers the shock of impact by breaking out of this pattern to punctuate with quotation marks. A number of subtle effects are generated by this finely nuanced grammar. One is to emphasize that what is important in the conversation is not what is said but how it is heard. The sentences are in solution with the receiving mind rather than under the authority of the speaker. How Mrs Ramsay and the eavesdropping James perceive Mr Ramsay's utterance is more important than what he is saying for its own sake. Reported speech mimes the fact that hearing a statement incorporates within the self, as part of the self, the reality of the thing said. We report messages to ourselves, as the mind interprets into the stuff of its own mental continuum the data supplied by the inner ear. As swallowed food transubstantiates into the being of the eater, so what we hear or read is assimilated and transformed. A second effect of this tendency of Virginia Woolf's technique of internalizing all experience is to comment on the apportionment of a single mind between two persons as a marital unit. To refuse quotation marks is to deny the boundary which segregates speech patterns into *meum* and *tuum*. The marriage of Mr and Mrs Ramsay, with all its tensions and inconsistencies, is projected in the book as capable of a wholeness of amity in which the need for words may be supererogatory. Intuitive understanding and the balm of mutual peace unforgettably evinced in the scene in which the couple read together (see pp. 27 ff.) exist as a ground of subconscious accord which superficial fluctuations fail to disturb. Reported speech in the scene of the quarrel implies the habituated and familial sharing of a mind, even while that mind is routinely at odds with itself. The quarrelsome corporate mind absorbs the systole–diastole motion of its dispute as an aspect of customary interplay. Mrs Ramsay is knitting, and the conversation has something of the regularity and conformity to pattern of that nearly automatic activity. 'But 'Damn you' bursts out of the continuum, splitting the shared mind into antagonized parts. 'Damn you' cannot be tolerated by the murmurous thought processes of life held in common.

This scrupulosity with the most minimal counters of verbal composition – pressure on listed words and phrases from emphatic semicolons (a favourite device); nuance of verb-tense; unusual inflections of meaning from the crafty withholding of quotation marks – signals the scale and certainty of the challenge Virginia Woolf is making to the medium of literary language, and her elaboration of its power to cast forth on to the page a fully internalized world. In her mature fiction,

CHESTER COLLEGE LIBRARY

reality is internalized because the external world is drained of verifiable reality. It cannot be known, only guessed, intuited, wished for or assumed. Minus this attribution, everything beyond our own eyes, ears and fingertips assumes a parlous character and becomes a matter for continuous debate, a process of ratiocination which can only reach conclusion with cessation of consciousness. Such oblivion, given the exacerbated state of self-consciousness which is represented as the human lot in *To the Lighthouse*, is often figured as desirable: the soft undertow of desire toward death. The lives Virginia Woolf mediates are those of over-stretched (metaphorical) insomniacs whose minds seldom switch off the long inquest on meaning, reality and relationship. People talk to themselves. Volleys of rhetorical questions start up from the depths of the spirit, one after another, and fall away aimlessly against the muffling walls of the self. In Virginia Woolf's world, there is no one to whom we may put these all-important questions: neither God, nor intermediary, nor wise man. The poet we might approach; but he (represented by Mr Carmichael) sleeps away his old age on the lawn in his own strange, cryptic stupor. Lily is most characteristically the mind which plays this fountain of rhetorical questions into the godless silence:

How then did it work out, all this? How did one judge people, think of them? How did one add up this and that and conclude that it was liking one felt, or disliking? And to those words, what meaning attached, after all? (p. 27)

What art was there, known to love or cunning, by which one pressed through into those secret chambers? What device for becoming, like waters poured into one jar, inextricably the same, one with the object one adored? Could the body achieve it, or the mind, subtly mingling in the intricate passages of the brain? or the heart? (p. 50)

She addressed old Mr Carmichael again. What was it then? What did it mean? Could things thrust their hands up and grip one; could the blade cut; the fist grasp? Was there no safety? No learning by heart of the ways of the world? No guide, no shelter, but all was miracle, and leaping from the pinnacle of a tower into the air? Could it be, even for elderly people, that this was life? – startling, unexpected, unknown? For one moment she felt that if they both got up, here, now on the lawn, and demanded an explanation, why was it so short, why was it so inexplicable, said it with violence, as two fully equipped human beings from whom nothing should be hid might speak, then, beauty would roll itself up, the space would fill, those empty flourishes would form into shape; if they shouted loud enough Mrs Ramsay would return. 'Mrs Ramsay!' she said aloud, 'Mrs Ramsay!' The tears ran down her face. (pp. 166–7)

Each pang of need and perplexity registers as a question mark. These are questions which no one will be able to answer for Lily, not only because they are those against which philosophy and religion have beaten their minds throughout the millennia, but also because Lily is not even able to frame them in words she could exchange with another person. We have learnt her private code of images and hence understand something of what she is asking when she wonders 'Could *things* thrust their *hands* up and grip one; could the *blade* cut; the *fist* grasp?' (my italics). 'What are these things with hands, this blade, this fist?' the man in the street might legitimately be expected to ask, looking askance at the embarrassing lady who speaks so oddly. The blade we divine as the Arthurian Sword Excalibur, the divinely talismanic key to meaning and power, held by the Lady of the Lake; but it is coated with modern and personal meanings, coded to Lily and her need for the all-explanatory mother-love that is submerged and drowned from her famishing, baffled eyes. This last, powerful build-up of rhetorical questions represents a climax of the novel, and a catharsis, for at last the gag on speech is torn away and Lily fills the space around her with invocatory voice: '"Mrs Ramsay! . . . Mrs Ramsay!"' We note that the great and terrible questions flung out rhetorically in the foregoing sentences ('What was it then? What did it mean?') dignified enough to be put by 'two fully equipped human beings' at the bar of the world, resolve themselves in the delivery to a sobbing cry for mother: the Mediatrix, Muse, Intercessor.

In *To the Lighthouse*, minds are overheard by us engaged in reverie, excogitation, uproars of rhetoric in which they silently castigate an imagined adversary, wince at imagined criticism or vindicate their way of seeing things. They muse, put this and that together, play with favourite or detested words. ('It was a splendid mind . . . his splendid mind . . . the letter Q. He reached Q . . . after Q? What comes next'? [p. 35]). The secretions of mental contents seethe through the circulation system with perpetual repetition. Mr Ramsay taps the key of *splendid* in his defensive fantasy of self-laudation, and then again *splendid*; and feels better, as if he has been adjudicated and not found wanting, but the effect of bolstering is transient, and he needs more and more of this unsatisfying fantasy-nutriment. With each tap of the key of *splendid* the text brings the word into fuller and fuller ironic focus. For Mr Ramsay's mind is 'splendid' but his vanity is more so. Compassion and amusement are both implied by the narrator's mimicry of Mr Ramsay's grapple with Q and R. 'If Q then is Q – R–' (p. 36). If the philosopher sticks at the first letter of his own name, R, we may surmise that the patriarchal code has failed to engage with the first premise of philosophy, the Delphic and Socratic 'Know yourself. Know that you know nothing'. *To the Lighthouse* may be said to *start* at the letter R, the letter of self-knowledge.

The novel as a whole is a profoundly reiterative document. Single words, phrases, grammatical constructions, whole sentences and configurations of sentences and paragraphs circulate in a variety of permutations. Key words or phrases will hold together an entire section, announcing themselves in the first paragraph, as in Mr Ramsay's assault on his wife's attentions ('There he stood, demanding sympathy' [p. 38]) to be repeated in every subsequent paragraph until he has attained his heart's desire. In Paragraph 2, 'He wanted sympathy . . . It was sympathy he wanted . . .', inverting the construction chiastically. In Paragraph 3, he is still not appeased, for 'He must have sympathy . . . again and again, demanding sympathy': *must* raises the pressure of demand, and the present participle, *demanding*, maintains it, the keyword *sympathy* concluding the paragraph. In Paragraph 4, *demanding sympathy* again concludes the paragraph, but desire is on the wane, and the gross adult suckling-babe drops from the breast replete: 'Filled with her words, like a child who drops off satisfied' (p. 40). One effect of this complex formulaic binding of narrative pattern upon significant words or phrases is to attribute to language a curious illusion of substantiality. Mr Ramsay comes to his wife holding the self wide open like a ravening mouth that imperatively must be fed. Its food will be the words he needs to hear in order to rest content. The whole episode reads like a metaphorical account of some physical exchange or intercourse, but in fact all Mrs Ramsay is doing is to hand over words, that light diet, evanescent as breath. Reading such a passage as this reminds us of how it feels to long for someone to say certain words, to be driven to exact such words of allegiance or fellow-feeling coercively. Such a transaction 'fills' the taker with 'her words' accompanied by a sensation of slight shame at his own antics, but sucks dry the giver, however willing, with a 'faintly disagreeable sensation' (p. 40). It is a curious reflection that these effects of psychological realism so acutely observed as to unnerve a reader, are a product of a technique as urbanely stylized and mannerist as this. Her concern to render the novel's language as a form of *poesis*, the creation of formal beauty, coincides with Virginia Woolf's close mimesis of the mind's verbal habits. The novel implies that we think in circles, writing round and round a palimpsest, inheritors of certain obsessive problems and a severely limited set of counters. The persons in the novel are problem-solving organisms, who put variations of a common problem to themselves in discrepant dialects, in terms of which they must also hazard solutions. Mr Ramsay's problem of the attainment of R is to Lily's ten-year search for the form of her picture what Mrs Ramsay's creation of harmony at the dinner-table is to Mr Bankes's search for scientific truth and Mr Carmichael's poetic inquiry. The quest is the same, for them as for the narrative voice: it is the establishment of a conviction or representation of 'a coherence in things, a stability; something . . . immune from change', as Mrs Ramsay figures it (p. 97). In the absence of this integrating principle, the mind – jostling items of perception like jigsaw pieces from a possible miscellany of puzzles – is disquiet. In momentary *aperçus*, the 'moments of being' which correspond in Virginia Woolf to Pater's burning moments or Joyce's epiphanies, this holistic integration of diversity is accomplished. Such moments feature sudden, revelatory experiences of insight into the unity of things, figured as visual images rather than abstract thoughts and hence not capable of translation into discursive or empirical language. *A Sketch of the Past* recounts a number of such instances experienced in her own life, each one as beautifully and economically composed as anything in her fiction, as if, in the case of these luminous moments, she could rely on the right words to accompany the remembrances as they surfaced into consciousness, swift and easy:

The second instance was also in the garden at St Ives. I was looking at the flower bed by the front door; 'That is the whole,' I said. I was looking at a plant with a spread of leaves; and it seemed suddenly plain that the flower itself was a part of the earth; that a ring enclosed what was the flower; and that was the real flower; part earth; part flower. It was a thought I put away as being likely to be very useful to me later. (p. 82)

In that wonderfully casual final sentence (Virginia 'puts away' as 'very useful' this image as a child stores for future use a remarkable feather or pebble in a drawer) she captures the *practical* importance of acts of meditative insight, for the making and sustaining of a whole life. This image of totality, rootedness and the essential fusion of source and created being is medicinable. To recur to it is to find healing ('whole', the key-word of the waking dream has a common root, in the Anglo-Saxon *hal*, with 'heal', 'hale') in an intuition not just of the interconnectedness of all things but of their fundamental identity. It also presents an abdication of linguistic usage for a perception of the 'real' which goes beyond language. For 'that was the real flower; part earth; part flower'. The narrow and codifying analytic tendencies of language are felt to direct attention to the part rather than the whole. Virginia Woolf's perception expands the 'real flower' to include what the language we inherit labels as 'not-a-flower', the sphere of encompassing earth, from which it has sprung, by which it is nourished, and to which it will return. Her novels search toward the creation of a holistic language able to body forth perceptions of this nature: the child in the mother, the present in the past, a sea of thought shared between boundaryless thinkers. In *To the Lighthouse*, such moments of vision which satisfy the mind with a sensation of the wholeness and plenitude of the perceived world are accompanied by an experience of completion and consummation, as well as a release of the lyricism which characterizes Virginia Woolf's style at moments of high emotion.

She was not quite accurate when she claimed in her Diary that 'The lyric portions of [*To the Lighthouse*] are collected in the 10 year lapse & don't interfere with the text so much as usual' (*Diary*, III, pp. 106–7, 5 September, 1926). Her singing voice was never as susceptible of such constraint. She has, typically, two manners, or modulations. One is a classical, rigorous Augustanism, which attends impeccably to the logic of its own grammar and the minutiae of behavioural representation; the other sings. *To the Lighthouse* achieves a more perfect harmony between the two poles than any other work. Except in the central Part, it is true, the Augustan manner is major, the lyric voice minor, but we will find examples of each on almost any page, and a middle style which fades the one into the other, through the subtle manipulations of the narrative voice:

Since he belonged, even at the age of six, to that great clan which cannot keep this feeling separate from that, *but* must let future prospects, with their joys *and* sorrows, cloud what is actually at hand, *since* to such people even in earliest childhood any turn in the wheel of sensation has the power to crystallize *and* transfix the moment upon which its gloom *or* radiance rests, James Ramsay, sitting on the floor cutting out pictures from the illustrated catalogue of the Army and Navy Stores, endowed the picture of a refrigerator as his mother spoke with heavenly bliss. (p. 9; my italics)

She was like a bird for speed, an arrow for directness. (p. 49)

The first sentence is bent on making a complex double distinction (predicated on the explanatory *since . . . since*) before it is willing to let the reader's inner voice and mind repose upon the main clause which opens on the name, *James Ramsay*, but even here it refuses rest and assurance by retentively withholding the completion of the main clause (*endowed the picture* . . .) until the very end of the sentence. This refusal to let the reader breathe easily by comforting him with an easy-going grammar can reach Miltonic proportions, not only by retarding the main verb and crowding the space of expectation with subordinate clauses (as in the classic 'Of man's first disobedience . . . Sing heavenly Muse' [*Paradise Lost*, I, 1–5]) but also by multiplying the main clause with half a page full of *and* or *yet* clauses; or – a vice of style since it reaches the edge of mannerism – the interpolation of actual or implied parentheses within a sentence, to record an external event simultaneous with interior monologue, or vice versa. Virginia Woolf is easy to parody; and difficult to write about without adopting her habitual inflections and rhetorical procedures, suits of clothes too strange and wonderful to fit any other mind but the original. The basis of the style which I have called the 'Augustan', taking its manner from Addison, Johnson, Swift and Jane Austen, depends on the making of distinctions, through antitheses, symmetry and balance of options or pairings, the incisive separation of *this* from *that* and the syllogistic drawing of conclusions from the distinction. The lyric voice does the opposite: it incants, invokes, suggests, moving toward emotional synthesis and an experience of wholeness of perception. However, it is worth noting that, in the first example, the complex description of James's disposition in terms of what it is not, employs its fastidious grammar of dissection to anatomize a disposition 'which cannot keep this feeling separate from that', that is, the content of the sentence ironically opposes its form.

Virginia Woolf identified the principle of rhythm as the foundation of her art, rather as Rebecca West focused on the sentence as the staple unit of composition. The Greeks accorded to *rhythmos* a creative primacy not only in poetry but in sculpture and architecture, reproducing a rhythmic cosmos in the proportioned curves of the human body in motion or the ratio between pillars in a temple. Virginia Woolf's neoclassicism (see pp. 105–12) in ascribing priority to rhythm casts it as the bearer-forth of meaning *ex nihilo*, an impulse of the voice which precedes image, vocabulary or thought. Her 'ear' is the structuring instrument in composition:

Could I get my tomorrow's rhythm right – take the skip of my sentence at the right moment – I should reel it off; . . . it's not style exactly – the right words – it's a way of levitating the thought out of one –

To appreciate this priority of rhythm in Virginia Woolf, the reader need only tell over a couple of her sentences, listening for qualities of voice rather than details of content. The sung quality of her sentences impresses the ear with the modulations of lyric poetry. Her explanation of the process of composition as 'levitating' the meaning out of herself gestures toward totality of effect and away from specificity of content; and yet we know her as one of the meticulous precision writers in our language, whose typical sentence incorporates a more than Jamesian fastidiousness of hair-splitting modification and annotation. But it is within this very elaboration (refusing to let the sentence die; holding on; interpolating behavioural description into the tracing of thought processes) that the 'levitating' 'skip' of her sentences paradoxically resides. The reading voice wants to subside; pause and start again. The Virginia Woolf sentence denies this lazy practice; commands not only flow but flight. It keeps urging the voice up, as in a long and searching elaboration of a theme in music, where the repeated phrases are both point of return and point of new departure. We can imagine setting some of these lyrical flights as poetry, scanning the stressed and unstressed syllables into subtle patterns, and even interpreting the frequent semicolons which both hold and impel the reading voice, as caesuras in poetry:

> Now she need not listen.
> It could not last she knew,
> but at the moment her eyes were so clear
> that they seemed to go round the table
> unveiling each of these people,
> and their thoughts and their feelings,
> without effort
> like a light stealing under water
> so that its ripples and the reeds in it
> and the minnows balancing themselves,
> and the sudden silent trout
> are all lit up
> hanging, trembling.
>
> (pp. 98–9)

The effect of setting her sentences thus is a visual recognition of the likeness of Virginia Woolf's prose in *To the Lighthouse* to the free verse, with its fluid variation on the basic rhythm of iambic pentameter, which was the form for modernistic experimental poetry in the twenties, from T. S. Eliot to Lawrence. The highly imagistic content displays techniques close to Imagism itself: binding devices such as alliteration (*ripples and the reeds*) and apparent duplications of grammatical structure which then break rhythm (*and the minnows ... and the sudden silent trout*) are the very stuff of modern poetry. The powerful stopping–starting device of semicolon as caesura may be exemplified in any one of dozens of sentences. At its simplest, the extravagant use of semicolon instructs the eye to pause and conceive of every item in a list as of significance in its own right:

Into [these waters] had spilled so many lives. The Ramsays'; the children's; and all sorts of waifs and strays of things besides. A washerwoman with her basket; a rook; a red-hot poker; the purples and grey-greens of flowers; some common feeling which held the whole together. (p. 177)

Withdraw the scoring of the passage which turns each listed item into the verbal equivalent of a phrase of music in a bar, and you are left with:

A washerwoman with her basket, a rook, a red-hot poker, the purples and grey-greens of flowers, some common feeling which held the whole together.

The function of the semicolon here is to wedge each phenomenon apart as requiring renewed attention, a rhythmic insistence which intensifies the reader's apprehension of the *thisness* of the object, its colour or its form. The flowers seem redder or more purple, the rook more creaturely, an effect we might perhaps compare with the testaments of the birds and insects in Gerard Manley Hopkins' sonnet, 'As kingfishers catch fire, dragonflies draw flame': *'Whát I dó is me: for that I came'* (line 8). The 'common feeling' which 'held the whole together' in the last line evokes, therefore, a more powerful sense of mystery in the garden's embrace of all these incompatibles. The weight of meaning and implication in these most minimal signs of articulation helps the reader to understand why the experience of reading Virginia Woolf can be so slow and fatiguing: the text's coercive demand is to be read with the finesse which wrote it, down to the last comma. The 'levitating' effects of the rhythmic manner are at their most exacting in a passage such as this at the dinner-party in which Mrs Ramsay's train of thought (in itself more than somewhat amorphous) is made to run on synchronously with an account of her hostly actions:

It partook, she felt, carefully helping Mr Bankes to a specially tender piece, of eternity; as she had already felt about something different once before that

53

afternoon; there is a coherence in things, a stability; something, she meant, is immune from change, and shines out (she glanced at the window with its ripple of reflected lights) in the face of the flowing, the fleeting, the spectral, like a ruby; so that again to-night she had the feeling she had had once to-day already, of peace, of rest. (p. 97)

The sentence contains nine clauses, four of which are main clauses, implying a new beginning. There are four semicolons, not necessarily coinciding with the main clauses and hence extending the number of points of impulsion, as does the parenthesis which rudely leaves the reader's voice hanging in mid-air, carrying the burden of the unfinished major clause while it directs attention elsewhere. A contrapuntal rhythmic principle (and new problems for the reader holding his breath) are provided by the mesmerizing repetitions of indeterminate words which require but cannot be supplied with explicit definition (*it . . . something . . . things . . . something*) so that the sentence always seems in pursuit of a code beyond the reach of words, in which lost cause it protracts itself as indefinitely as possible. A verbal impressionism which incants suggestive possibilities (*the flowing, the fleeting, the spectral, like a ruby*) draws the long sentence to a lullaby conclusion (*of peace, of rest*) like a painfully wordy mind which shuts down its monotonous soliloquy only to sleep.

Related to the rhythmic energies which carry the novel forward, we find uniquely in *To the Lighthouse* a language which attributes sensual properties to mental processes. Characters in *To the Lighthouse* scarcely ever touch. They watch. They do not embrace – though Lily once, extraordinarily and inconclusively, 'laid her head on Mrs Ramsay's lap and laughed' (p. 50). They stand or sit aside, attentive to their own mental functions. Paul and Minta do kiss, an event which the text ultimately identifies (in the failure of the marriage) as a mistake. Otherwise, sensual functions are limited to reading, eating and enjoying the thought or image of beauty. And yet our experience is that this is a passionate novel. We are responding, I think, to the wholesale transference of libido from bodily to mental functions. As a result of this suppression and displacement of desire, we witness in the novel the sexualization of the mental life or the cerebration of sexuality. The most obvious such scene is that in which Mr Ramsay remorselessly plunges the 'beak of brass' into Mrs Ramsay's 'delicious fecundity', with the incensed child James 'stiff between her legs' at his father's assault (pp. 38–9). The scene is projected as a violent phallic penetration and appropriation of the female life-force, a close approximation to the reiterative thrusting of the sexual act, its 'rapture' (p. 40) connoting an element of rape and its faintly disgusted aftermath carrying post-coital suggestions. And yet all the characters are actually doing is talking, and one of them is actually knitting (rather fast).

However, events more subtle than this isolated set-piece, which compose the basic thought-line of the novel, gain their imagistic intensity from this displacement of libido. Tension is made to build in a character's mind as she – say, Lily, testing Mr Bankes over against Mr Ramsay – agitates over irreconcilable hypotheses, 'saying without prompting undeniable, everlasting, contradictory things' (p. 27):

All of this danced up and down, like a company of gnats, each separate, but all marvellously controlled in an invisible elastic net – danced up and down in Lily's mind, in and about the branches of the pear tree, where still hung in effigy the scrubbed kitchen table, symbol of her profound respect for Mr Ramsay's mind, until her thought which had spun quicker and quicker exploded of its own intensity; she felt released; a shot went off close at hand, and there came, flying from its fragments, frightened, effusive, tumultuous, a flock of starlings. (p. 28)

The sentence structure dramatizes in its longevity and yet its whirling rapidity the pace of Lily's unbearable need for her own thought to break and resolve, borne up and kept there by the familiar devices of rhythmic repetition (*up and down* ... *in and about*), and modifying clauses loaded with symbolic connotation, until the sentence signals its climax on *until* and explodes upon the verb *explode*. The sudden release of tension is, characteristically, marked by an image – the shot, and spasmic flight of starlings, with the violent insinuation of menace which articulates a horror always, for Virginia Woolf, latent in sexual experience and its mental counterpart. Such mimesis, far from being an occasional effect of the novel, supplies a principle of its structural movement. Thought is all there is of body in *To the Lighthouse*: the corporeality attributed to thought allows the author to figure forth processes which we as readers can recognize as universal in the mind's rhythms. Exquisite moments of insight when the outside world seems to pour into the skull as a sea of brilliant colour and textures are especially susceptible of this method of representing the mind as if it were a sentient organism. Mrs Ramsay watches the hypnotic lighthouse beam 'with fascination':

she looked at the steady light, the pitiless, the remorseless, which was so much her, yet so little her, which had her at its beck and call (she woke in the night and saw it bent across their bed, stroking the floor), but for all that she thought, watching it with fascination, hypnotized, as if it were stroking with its silver fingers some sealed vessel in her brain whose bursting would flood her with delight, she had known happiness, exquisite happiness, intense happiness, and it silvered the rough waves a little more brightly, as daylight faded, and the blue went out of the sea and it rolled in waves of pure lemon which curved and swelled and broke upon the beach and the ecstasy burst in her eyes and waves of pure delight raced over the floor of her mind and she felt, It is enough! It is enough! (pp. 62–3)

It is a curious paradox that the author who has uniquely forced the solid body of English prose through the needle's eye of her own denial of corporeality, has transferred to the mind, to an almost embarrassing degree, bodily functions, needs and issues. Her writing covers our guesswork of other people's thought processes (which are pure inference for we cannot see, hear or share them) with a kind of verbal ectoplasm, which takes a form the senses *can* conceive. The sensual effects of the passage in which Mrs Ramsay's eyes meet the revelatory lighthouse beam are intense to the point of unpleasantness on the reader's nerve-endings. The prose moves through a pun on *strokes* as 'rhythmic movement' and 'fondling sensation' to the extraordinarily tactile image of 'some sealed vessel in her brain', imagined as a sac filled with liquid and ultra-responsive to stimulation. This strange anatomical organ suggests perhaps a womb in the mind, whose bursting resembles the rupture of the membrane to break the waters at birth. Or, as one reads on, and 'the ecstasy burst in her eyes and waves of pure delight raced over the floor of her mind', one conceives a sort of orgasm-in-the-eye. Colour is mediated as hallucinogenic (the lemon-yellow sea), time as speeded up like the fast flow of a film (mimed by swift phrases linked only by *and . . . and . . . and*). The experience implies a violent, discomforting Keatsianism of sensastion (To 'burst Joy's grape against his palate fine' (*Ode on Melancholy*, line 27) and an alien internal geography of the human interior corresponding to the later visionary guesswork of Dylan Thomas: 'Light breaks where no sun shines,/ Where no seas run the waters of the heart/ Push in their tides' (*Light breaks*, lines 1–3).

For Virginia Woolf, language itself is infinitely problematic. It is all we have to communicate with and to record, criticize and extend our knowledge of reality, but it is a vagrant, equivocal and self-referring medium. Language can interpose between the reality it alleges and the eyes that search it out, mystifying rather than revealing. In *Mrs Dalloway* she set forth her doubts not only as to the arcane character of what we see in the world and its mysterious susceptibility to plurality of interpretation but also as to the legibility of words themselves. Two test cases are given. A car travels down Bond Street and ripples speculation in the crowd: some identify the portentous occupant as the Queen, others the Prince of Wales, the Prime Minister, a refraction of the Almighty himself. An aeroplane advertises some product with a trail of smoky letters across the sky. London looks up and begins corporately to decode the obscure letters:

> But what letters? A C was it? an E, then an L? Only for a moment did they lie still; then they moved and melted and were rubbed out up in the sky, and the aeroplane shot further away and again, in a fresh space of sky, began writing a K, and E, a Y perhaps?
>
> 'Blaxo,' said Mrs Coates in a strained, awe-stricken voice . . .
>
> 'Kreemo,' murmured Mrs Bletchley . . .
>
> 'That's an E,' said Mrs Bletchley . . .
>
> 'It's toffee,' murmured Mr Bowley . . .
>
> So, thought Septimus, looking up, they are signalling to me. Not indeed in actual words; that is, he could not read the language yet; but it was plain enough, this beauty . . . (*Mrs Dalloway*, pp. 24–5)

You read BLAXO, I read KREEMO, he reads messages from the gods in a language as yet unrevealed. The sky is inscribed with competing airborne texts all founded for the curious reader on exactly the same letters – 'But what letters?' With elegant, charitable mockery, Virginia Woolf focuses on the straining eyes of the earthbound people deciphering a version of reality which they expect to see, and none more madly than another, for Septimus (though labelled 'madman') at least acknowledges himself to be as yet unversed in the language. The author even provides an ironic key to her code, literally building it into her transcription of variant interpretations: 'began writing a K, and E, a Y perhaps': KEY. Some such key had been available to previous generations in the Book of Nature, signed with God's meaningful emblems and read with the eye of right reason, on the one hand, and the Book of God, the Scriptures, on the other, a hermeneutic guide. God's handwriting on the material universe, instinct with messages and signs, could be evaluated and expounded in a language founded on the creating Word. Virginia Woolf records a modern world in which to impute creativity to words (Septimus's Orphic claim that 'the human voice . . . can quicken trees into life!' [p. 26]); to think of the world as revelatory (p. 29); to take messages at the Divine Dictation and to perceive meaning and pattern flowing through all things (p. 26) qualifies the individual for hospitalization. Divine hallucinations are estranging and stigmatizing, where the general norm is to read messages off the top of one's head (BLAXO, KREEMO, KEY) and relate them straight back into the materialistic solipsism of day-to-day expectation.

Yet *Mrs Dalloway* and, even more so, *To the Lighthouse* testify to their author's suspicion that, just beyond the capacity of language to express it, lay some transcendent meaning, or ontological certainty, or Being (none of these words quite suit, but that is precisely because words come laden with centuries of previous connotation and, cleaving in a network to one another, cannot find new targets of definition). *To the Lighthouse* presents intimations of what it cannot, by its very nature as a work of words, define or describe. In the Diaries, Virginia Woolf recurrently mentions a curious mental phenomenon which she is unable to specify in language. During the writing of *To the Lighthouse*, she described one instance thus:

... I have some restless searcher in me. Why is there not a discovery in life? Something one can lay hands on & say 'This is it?' My depression is a harassed feeling – I'm looking; but that's not it – that's not it. What is it? And shall I die before I find it? Then (as I was walking through Russell Square last night) I see the mountains in the sky: the great clouds; & the moon which is risen over Persia; I have a great & astonishing sense of something there, which is 'it' – It is not exactly beauty that I mean. It is that the thing is in itself enough: satisfactory; achieved. A sense of my own strangeness, walking on the earth is there too: of the infinite oddity of the human position; trotting along Russell Square with the moon up there, & those mountain clouds. Who am I, what am I, & so on: these questions are always floating about in me; & then I bump against some exact fact – a letter, a person, & come to them again with a great sense of freshness. And so it goes on. But, on this showing which is true, I think, I do fairly frequently come upon this 'it'; & then feel quite at rest. (*Diary*, III, pp. 62–3)

This wonderfully unsatisfying description of the moment of insight rests upon the scruple under which it lays itself of refusing the familiar labels which cover rather than disclose the meaning of what is experienced: 'God', 'beauty', 'harmony', 'acceptance', 'mother'. The *it*, ten times reiterated, the *Ding-an-sich* which is apprehended, can be suggested only dimly through spectacle (the cloudbank, the moonscape), giving a sense of human diminution in the magnified cosmos, and through the sequence of thought-events which flow from this perception of whatever-it-is. The passage stresses neither the familiar 'rapture' nor 'ecstasy' of *To the Lighthouse* but an emotion more grounded and low-key: rest and relief, as we may feel when something we have mislaid – or someone – which was on the tip of one's tongue and just around the corner, is located: a brooch on the sea-shore, the whereabouts of mother. There is a sense of completion, accompanied by a sigh of relief which comes when a work of art has been finished (Lily's 'It was done; it was finished' at the end of *To the Lighthouse* [p. 192]), or a sequence of thoughts, a labour or a life has been brought to a conclusion (Mrs Ramsay's 'It is enough, it is enough' [p. 63]; Mrs McNab's 'it was finished' [p. 131]). It is notably what Mr Ramsay, fretted, self-pitying, insecure, cannot achieve when he sticks on Q:

Then R . . . He braced himself. He clenched himself . . .

R is then – what is R? . . .

On to R, once more. R – . . .

Meanwhile, he stuck at Q. On, then, on to R . . .

He would never reach R. (pp. 36–7)

Mr Ramsay charges at the invincible R like the entire Light Brigade, doing and dying, and flounders at the end of each successive paragraph humiliated before a dash or a question mark, goading his already galled brain – a discomfort at being stuck, unable to complete a quest whose familiarity to every reader is signalled in the rueful fellow-feeling which accompanies the exposure to laughter in the text's irony. *To the Lighthouse* is, as its title implies, a quest novel. The lighthouse is a focus of desire and value as mythically magnetizing as the Grail to Sir Galahad, Ithaka to Odysseus or the Hesperidean Islands to mainland Greece. As the eye of the younger Catherine is drawn to the 'bare masses of stone . . . bright so long after it is evening here' (Emily Brontë, *Wuthering Heights*, Ch. 18), her maternal inheritance of the 'eternal rocks beneath', so James Ramsay, his mother's child, sailing in toward the white, stark tower rooted in the rock sees the source of the winking eye and knows 'So that was the Lighthouse, was it? . . . No, the other was also the Lighthouse' (p. 172). It is a zone of interest made sacred by the premium that is put on it by the novel, a forcefield of meaning which words cannot cover. The meaning of the Lighthouse cannot be told by the characters in the novel or by the narrative voice. It is written around, preserved as mystery, like the unknowable R, or like Virginia Woolf's own experience of 'something there, which is "it"' (see p. 58).

The physical actuality of the lighthouse, as the Ramsays' boat nears it, resembles nothing in literature as resonantly as Milton's Paradise after the fall, moved 'by might of waves':

> Down the great river to the opening gulf,
> And there take root an island salt and bare,
> The haunt of seals and orcs, and sea-mews' clang.
> (*Paradise Lost*, XI. 830, 833–5)

The temperate fertile zone, dragged up by the roots and discharged to the bitter maritime weathers, cleansed of human habitation, is a terrible image of purgation, haunted by the rough elegy of bird calls and the human-headed seals. The 'island salt and bare' on which the lighthouse is located has something of this character of a memorial or obelisc, after the Deluge, a place that is sacred to the book where questors might go as now they do to Holy Island, to a long-vacated shrine open to all weathers.

'I do fairly frequently come upon this "it"; and then feel quite at rest' (p. 58). To attain *fairly frequently* the quiet consummation of this mental satisfaction is to be a fairly frequent visitor to the house of light. It is one of the lovelier touches of *To the Lighthouse* that Virginia Woolf allows only to the figure of the father, so much rebuked and ironized, to follow to its quietus the signpost by which the novel's title directs its persons and readers to the end of the quest: – To the Lighthouse:

He rose and stood in the bow of the boat, very straight and tall, for all the world, James thought, as if he were saying, 'There is no God,' and Cam thought, as if he were leaping into space, and they both rose to follow him as he sprang, lightly like a young man, holding his parcel, on to the rock. (pp. 190–1)

'"He must have reached it," said Lily' (p. 191). That is, he has reached *it*. With the parcel which signifies his belated, faithful fulfilment of Mrs Ramsay's errand, Mr Ramsay's spring 'into space' impersonates the Kierkegaardian free leap into the unknown arms of the living God, at the end of the world. It is an image which gestures both toward the achievement of life's completion in death, and towards transformation and reunion, for Mr Ramsay leaps 'lightly like a young man', sloughing the decrepitude of age as if to participate in those regenerative nature myths to which the author has assimilated the figure of the mother. He alone reaches the other side, the fulfilment of the quest, leaving the two children saluting him in their hearts, forever poised to follow him from the boat: the young waiting in the wake of the recessional older generation. No voice tells us so, in so many words, but our impression – gathered from the slant implications of the composition of symbols, images, literary and mythological allusions and a language which always seems to mean more than it will say – is that, as Mr Ramsay takes this final leap to journey's end, he goes over the threshold into death, willingly; and we, as well as his children, renounce him willingly, having the presentiment that he reaches R, and Mrs Ramsay.

The intimation of a cryptic, transcendent reality just beyond the horizon of language, and out of reach of the five senses, is intensely present in the shimmering suggestiveness of its narrative voice as it searches out the means of its quest, to cast over an indefinable quarry the net of language. 'One could not say what one meant', thinks Lily in Part One, attempting to categorize her strong attraction to Mrs Ramsay and the world she centres (p. 23). In Part Three she is no nearer to discovering the words which will furnish a key to her most preoccupying and elusive inquiries:

But one only woke people if one knew what one wanted to say to them. And she wanted to say not one thing, but everything. Little words that broke up the thought and dismembered it said nothing. 'About life, about death; about Mrs Ramsay' – no, she thought, one could say nothing to nobody. The urgency of the moment always missed its mark. Words fluttered sideways and struck the object inches too low. Then one gave it up; then the idea sunk back again . . . (p. 165)

The limitations of language as committed to partiality and the accumulation of fragments of meaning are a product of its existence in time. Lily sees words as breaking down rather than building up meaning (the 'idea' being a living body which articulation 'dismembers'). Because language – unlike the visual arts – is a linear process of sounds, or the signs for such sounds, in time, so that we are either awaiting the completion of meaning or have passed it by, it is the least adapted of artistic agents to mediate the holistic sense of 'everything'. It is a strictly mortal code. Yet this mortal measure has the dubious glory of uttering negatives, dissatisfactions, losses and incompleteness to perfection: it speaks volumes about its own inadequacy. 'No, she thought one could say *nothing* to *nobody*' (my emphases). In Lily's parlance, the double negative fails to add up to a positive by managing to imply the presence in the world of 'nobodies' to whom one could impart 'nothing' on a day-to-day basis. Lily's image of the over-eager archer whose ill-judged arrow floats out of true is an image of the built-in failure of aspiration in a discouraging world in which, Platonistically, the soul is condemned to seek its proper desire through a medium of sluggish corporeality. In the end, language seems to collapse into a cry of need for all that we don't have and cannot call into being:

> To want and not to have ... And then to want and not to have – to want and want – how that wrung the heart, and wrung it again and again! Oh Mrs Ramsay! she called out silently, to that essence ... (p. 165)

> 'Mrs Ramsay! Mrs Ramsay!' she cried, feeling the old horror come back – to want and want and not to have. (p. 186)

Language turns back into the high-pulse, tearing cries of infancy, its range of meanings simplified into a call for the filling of this empty, unaccompanied self which only knows that, if it is to survive, its elementary hungers must somehow be accommodated. This is an 'old' horror: archaic, pre-historic, known by the self before language was known – *want* ... *want* ... *want*, the burden of Tennyson's self-stigmatization as 'An infant crying in the night ... And with no language but a cry' (*In Memoriam*, LIV, also see pp. 14–15).

In *To the Lighthouse* language is a subject of the novel: its limitations, its miraculous fabulations, its detachability from the objects and experiences it is supposed to denote. Language is given a kind of visual being, so that it takes on an illusion of colour, shape, texture and substantiality. The whole text is a field of imagery in which language is also realized in pictorial form. Virginia Woolf's mind has a peculiar and thrilling doubleness. It is at once the most abstracting and the most teemingly visual of imaginations. Leonard Woolf recalled how the speech of his wife, in conversation, would suddenly begin to fountain with visual images; a flood of extraordinary visualizations would arrest her listeners as if summoned as guests into someone's colourful dream. Her written language has the same pictorial roots, signing each referent in terms of a picture, or pictogram of some other visible object. Thinking of poetry, Mrs Ramsay conceives that 'words, like little shaded lights, one red, one blue, one yellow, lit up in the dark of her mind' (p. 109). In *To the Lighthouse* there is an investiture of nakedly abstract ideas with visual correspondences, which in their turn gesture toward a meaning beyond the visual. The novel draws attention to its own words, asking us to test their light and colour against our inner screen, and to consider their beauty for its own sake. We may think of *To the Lighthouse* as a meditation on Beauty – both that of a person

(Mrs Ramsay's 'incomparable beauty which she lived behind' [p. 31]) and that of a work of art. Her English has been called mannered, precious, mandarin as opposed to the demotic prose style of her rival and friend, Katherine Mansfield, and it is not unfair to remind ourselves that during her formative years the art-for-art's-sake movement was in its heyday. The inheritance of Pater and Wilde is there in her concern for formal qualities of style, poise, elegance and finesse in the compositon of each phrase and sentence, but the manuscript of each novel was laid as a thin film across the abyss, and she speaks in a beautiful voice of terrible, threatening experiences, not to falsify or wish them away but to bring within the compass of beauty and our willing contemplation realities in themselves too ugly for sustained meditation.

To the Lighthouse maintains that there may be perception without language. Lily's eyes fill with 'a hot liquid (she did not think of tears at first)' (p. 166). The withholding of the verbal label adeptly catches the immediacy of involuntary action. The tear scalds the eye with a surprising suddenness and is registered in the narrative the moment before it is translated into the conventionalizing common tongue, stressing how little we know or can predict our deepest emotional responses and behaviour. The word 'tear' is made to seem a cipher superadded to the reality, from a code which does not quite fit human events in the form they are experienced, the tear-in-the-eye, the sound-in-the-ear. The novel makes a long and crafty sequence of raids on simultaneity, seeking to bring the words closer in to the experience, minimizing the time gap which intervenes between the thing perceived and its encapsulation as meaning. Again and again, the narrative voice reports the frustration of this inconsistency, the fleetingness and fluency of impressions and the hampering stride of the mind 'following a voice which speaks too quickly to be taken down by one's pencil' (p. 27). Through the person of Lily in her earnest, loving, baffled search to get out of her the inspirations that are locked up in her, Virginia Woolf provides us with a running commentary on her own difficulties and pleasures in writing *To the Lighthouse*, in solving the heady conundrum of using language to signify intuitions that are, by their very nature, beyond language.

Ultimately, *To the Lighthouse* must rank as one of the world's great magician's tricks: sleight of hand and *trompe-l'oeil* undertaken self-deprecatingly, with that profoundly false modesty of which Virginia Woolf was an ironic past master, and carried out in a mood of triumph. Each Part ends on an up-beat, contradicting the dying fall on which each seems intent: Part One ends *triumphed again*; Part Two *Awake*, the call to *Reveille*; Part Three a final triumph *I have had my vision*. For T. S. Eliot in *The Waste Land*, which she and Leonard Woolf had published at the Hogarth Press three years previously, the inadequacy of Western language and culture is circumvented by the invocation of the authoritative thunder of an exotic language's onomatopoeia – the assonances and alliterations of the *Upanishad*'s imperatives: 'Datta. Dayadhvam. Damyata./ Shantih shantih shantih' (V. 432). Virginia Woolf's strategies are more subtle, equivocal and reticent. They involve the camouflage of one art in another. Eliot resolves his poem on a report of 'What the thunder said'; Virginia Woolf her elegy on a mimesis of 'What the paint said'. She can tell us in literary language what Lily painted, with such delicate suggestiveness that we can close the book and replace it on the shelf curiously convinced that we have 'seen' Lily's picture. For we have lived with its 'triangular purple shape, "just there"' (p. 52), the problem of the position of the tree and how it might be brought into more satisfying relationship to the devious middle-ground (p. 87), the difficulty of painting an evacuated sitter and her imaginary reinstatement in the field of vision, conjured from the void by the painter's concentrated, worshipping love – 'There she sat' (p. 186) – and the drawing of the final line, for the literary equivalent of ten years. We often say that the novelist 'paints', 'depicts', 'sketches', 'delineates' or 'portrays' his subject, demonstrating our submission to the primacy of the visual in all human conceptualizations: *I see* for *I understand*. Virginia Wolf 'paints' the painter painting. She presents a literary mimesis of an artistic mimesis of the abstract essence of the group portrait of mother, son, tree and home, and in so doing can assimilate the time-enthralled medium of language to the atemporality of visual art. By insisting on Lily's picture as an *abstract* composition, she can further imply that a 'reality' behind imagery has been called into focus on our behalf, hesitantly, bafflingly, by a pen which fabricates the illusions of a brush. We are more beguiled by this illusionism than by Henry James's *Portrait of a Lady* or James Joyce's *Portrait of the Artist as a Young Man*, since here we are invited to share the act of creative vision moment by moment, and to participate, reading the story of Lily's picture over her shoulder and reproducing a personal version of it on the canvas of the imagination. The heavy use of indeterminate words (*it, something, things, life*) also acts to exploit the inadequacy of language by opening meaning to be supplied by the reader's imagination:

Beneath *it* is all dark, *it* is all spreading, *it* is unfathomably deep; but now and again we rise to the surface and that is what you see us by. (p. 60)

There was in Lily a thread of *something*; a flare of *something*; *something* of her own . . . (p. 96, [my italics])

In these momentary engagements with this *something* (that which the central section's events seek to disprove, and bring to nothing), there is a sense of peaceful affirmation, a faith in the unconscious and language-less sources of self as meaningful plenitudes which we intuit and need not try to prove.

3. The Question of the Table

We can imagine a twentieth-century artist – Picasso, say, or Matisse – deciding to take as the subject of his picture a homely kitchen table. Vermeer would have stood it foursquare on a chequered kitchen floor like a draughts' board under the light from a high window; a woman might have stood alongside reading a letter, and we would wonder what news it brought that made for such a stillness beside the solid table. Gainsborough's table would have been an expensive and elegant piece of property, exquisitely inlaid and silken-surfaced like the lady who graced it with her more costly person. But Picasso and Matisse would question the table rigorously, plucking it out of its consensus use and expectation and appropriating it into inner space. Is there any reason, they might ask, spinning the idea of the table in their minds, why this object should be represented as standing on its four legs in a kitchen, cravenly subservient to bourgeois conventions? Tables have four legs but so do creatures: let it walk off into its own world of time and space. Let us up-end it and send it sailing from the indoor world where it is more normally approached, out to a place where people can really think about it. In a tree, for instance, its original source, the artefact of culture may be returned to nature, and what we have appropriated may be reassigned to the status of rooted wood. Or, they might have reflected, let us carve the table up into sixty-two different geometrical parts and fit them back together as collage. Since, after all, there is no objectively 'real table' but only our delusive but challenging sense-impressions to testify to what lies out there, the artist is free to offer his own experimental account of his mental contents tossed out upon the field of vision. So also Lily Briscoe, the artist of *To the Lighthouse*, conceives a table disobedient to the laws of nature and reason, and hangs it in a pear tree in the Ramsays' garden:

So she always saw, when she thought of Mr Ramsay's work, a scrubbed kitchen table. It lodged now in the fork of a pear tree, for they had reached the orchard. And with a painful effort of concentration, she focused her mind, not upon the silver-bossed bark of the tree, or upon its fish-shaped leaves, but upon the phantom kitchen table, one of those scrubbed board tables, grained and knotted, whose virtue seems to have been laid bare by years of muscular integrity, which stuck there, its four legs in air. Naturally, if one's days were passed in this seeing of angular essences, this reducing of lovely evenings, with all their flamingo clouds and blue and silver to a white deal four-legged table (and it was a mark of the finest minds to do so), naturally one could not be judged like an ordinary person. (p. 26)

Lily has wondered what Mr Ramsay's books were about, and been told by his son that they concerned '"Subject and object and the nature of reality"'. Lily declared herself still at a loss, and received the further explanation: '"Think of a kitchen table then ... when you're not there"'. This was what catapulted the table into the tree.

Virginia Woolf's technique in estranging the Idea of the Table so far from its home in the comfortable continuum of empirical reality closely resembles the devices and desires of modern art, where mental contents deposit themselves spatially wherever you happen to be, as images amongst images. Stuck in the fork of the pear tree, Mr Ramsay's object of thought as conceived by Lily looks spectacularly foolish, inverted and displaying all four legs like an animal, the furniture not of use but of thought, but for all that an object of reverence. The delicate irony which at once judges and defends all the persons of *To the Lighthouse* is exquisitely balanced here to evoke a mood of wry admiration for Mr Ramsay's pursuit of the *vita contemplativa*. Lily's trustful, amused parenthesis '(and it was a mark of the finest minds to do so)' at once satirizes the pure unadulterated uselessness of applying one's mind to essences abstracted from particulars and celebrates the lonely vocation of the life of thought. Of course, Lily cannot actually 'see' anything like the 'table' Mr Ramsay has in mind when he applies himself to the problems of 'subject and object and the nature of reality'. Lily's table has a vivid particularity which marks it as hers and no other's. First of all, it has been 'scrubbed' over a period of years by some woman's arm, whose 'muscular integrity' gestures forward to the work of renovation accomplished by the cleaning ladies of Part Two: the practical labours of the *vita activa*, whose strenuous activities do in some strange way complement the work of thought which is the profession of the philosopher. Mrs Bast's table is there for utility; Mr Ramsay's and Lily's are rescued from their utility, but Lily's vision opposes Mr Ramsay's by concerning itself with semblances. His, no doubt, is set in vacant space and slimmed down to its basic geometry; hers is 'grained and knotted' with its own characterful handwriting, with a history of associations. Yet, with one of those arresting paradoxes in which *To the Lighthouse* delights, Lily is an abstract artist whose own quest is the reduction of the objects of perception to their 'angular essences', if the 'triangular

67

purple shadow' which denotes Mrs Ramsay and James in her picture is anything to go by.

The question of the table is a major preoccupation not only of the thinking people in the novel but also of the novel itself. *To the Lighthouse* is a thinking organ which sets itself the task of contemplating 'subject and object and the nature of reality', by approaching the threshold between *what I am* and *what I see*, scanning the eye-beam that claims to link the two and investigating the channel of hearing that delivers the speaker to the hearer. Dr Johnson's response to the subjectivists' query as to how we can verify the reality of the empirical universe was the practical injunction to kick the stone, and if the stone moved and your foot hurt, the stone was real and so was your foot. The novel cannot take aim at the stone. The writer by the very nature of his trade has his eyes down and cannot keep track of material nature, being therefore condemned to submit to Andrew Ramsay's suggestion to '"Think of a kitchen table then ... *when you're not there*"' (my emphasis added). Absence and loss are at the heart of this elegiac novel: literally, at the centre, which covers the anguish of having to think of tables, beds, gloves, carpets, books, the entire paraphernalia of the human home, and the home itself, *when you're not there*. The narrative voice bears impersonal witness to the unspeakable and (literally) invisible vision of a domestic world emptied of human content. It is part of the novel's extraordinary virtuosity to encompass this literal impossibility: turning its back, to claim that no human eyes are inspecting the scene of the abdicated house, but observing what is transpiring (or failing to transpire) behind in a covert mirror of its own devising.

To the most robust human ego it comes as a recurrent shock that things can go on without our being conscious of them, as if our presence or awareness of events were necessary to authorize and validate them. This attachment to our indispensability as arbiters of reality is a testament to the difficulty (registered by all the protagonists of *To the Lighthouse*) of renouncing the belief in the self as centring the sphere of meaningful reality. Mrs Ramsay is mortified at her dinner party to receive Mr Bankes's news of an old friend after whom she asks:

And was Carrie still living at Marlow, and was everything still the same? (p. 82)

But how strange, she repeated, to Mr Bankes's amusement, that they should be going on there still. For it was extraordinary to think that they had been capable of going on living all these years when she had not thought of them more than once all that time. How eventful her own life had been, during those same years. Yet perhaps Carrie Manning had not thought about her either. The thought was strange and distasteful. (p. 83)

The unpleasant taste in Mrs Ramsay's mind as she gets a mirror-glimpse of the autonomy of circles beyond her organizing power decreases her own sense of reality, and devalues her own history which has appropriated twenty-year-old events and stabilized a memory of them as part of herself. Her ego's cry against change ('No! No! That was out of the question! Building a billiard room!' [p. 82]) corresponds to a cry of the author in the novel as she confronts ruinous change to the sanctities of a childhood home in 'Time Passes'. The perception here is close to that figured in George Eliot's famous 'pier-glass' analogy in *Middlemarch*:

Your pier-glass or extensive surface of polished steel made to be rubbed by a housemaid, will be minutely and multitudinously scratched in all directions; but place now against it a lighted candle as a centre of illumination, and lo! the scratches will seem to arrange themselves in a fine series of concentric circles round that little sun. It is demonstrable that the scratches are going everywhere impartially, and it is only your candle which produces the flattering illusion of a concentric arrangement, its light falling with an exclusive optical selection. These things are a parable. The scratches are events, and the candle is the egoism of any person now absent – of Miss Vincy, for example. (p. 297)

In each case, the principle labelled with a characteristic show of scientific omniscience by George Eliot as 'an exclusive optical selection' stands in a parabolic relation to the story as a whole. However, Virginia Woolf – her narrative perception being subject to the same limitations and obscurities as the persons amongst whom she is diffused – does not urge her parable as a moral adjudication of the egoisms it exposes; rather as symptomatic of the metaphysical difficulties that stand in the way of a stable sense of self in the volatile seas of experience which surround the individual, and are mostly off the horizon of vision. We feel most acutely when reading Virginia Woolf the inadequacy of our predicament – being born with only the one pair of eyes and ears to feed with glimpses and hearsay the sequestered mind within the skull, as puzzled as Malvolio in his Egyptian darkness. The implicated narrative voice does not claim for itself better optical instruments than the hazards, guessworks, leaps of faith or intuition and circular ratiocinations of the persons it mimes.

During the 1920s, Virginia Woolf was reading Plato and responding intensely to his inquiry into the relation between 'subject and object and the nature of reality'. In 1908, the notebooks report that she read the *Symposium*, (and again in 1920) and the *Phaedrus*, in 1923 *Euthyphro*, in 1924 *Protagoras*. Her entire career can be viewed as an attempt to locate the exit from Plato's cave of the senses to the transcendent reality of the Ideas or Forms; to quit the delusive half-light where the shadows of images held between a fire and a wall are the only available (and consensus) versions of reality (*Republic*, VII, 514A–521B). The minds whose flickerings and candle-lit guessing-games we view in *To the Lighthouse* resemble this wall of Plato's cave as it dances with phantasmal imagery. It is her most deeply and consistently Platonist work. Virginia Woolf's 'table' belongs to the same workshop as Plato's 'bed'. In the *Republic*, Socrates instructs the unfortunate Glaucon on the question of the Ideal (god-made) Bed, the manufactured bed upon which one sleeps (a copy of the original), and the painter's representation of a bed (a copy of a copy):

> And we may call the carpenter the manufacturer of a bed?
> Yes.
> Can we say the same of the painter?
> Certainly not.
> Then what is he, with reference to a bed?
> I think it would be fairest to describe him as the artist who represents the things which the other two make.
> Very well, said I; so the work of the artist is at the third remove from the essential nature of the things?
> Exactly.
> The tragic poet, too, is an artist who represents things; so this will apply to him: he and all other artists are, as it were, third in succession from the throne of truth.
> Just so. (*Republic*, X, 597)

The ignominious status accorded to the poet by Plato as the third-rate fabricator of illusions is tested out by Virginia Woolf in *To the Lighthouse* by presenting the artist (Lily) as concerned with abstraction, rather than with verisimilitude. The subject of her picture, the mother-and-child icon, is presented as reachable in its essence rather than its appearance, 'reduced', as Lily explains to Mr Bankes in Part One, 'to a purple shadow without irreverence' (p. 52). Through this dextrous manoeuvre, pressure on which is sustained throughout the novel, art is made to seem able to short-circuit the chain of degenerate images which blocks Reality from the inner eye, by the application of the classic

Neoplatonist riposte to Plato: art does not lie because it is conscious 'feigning'; connects with Truth by painting not semblances but 'the Idea' itself (Sidney, *Defence of Poetry*, p. 79).

In the *Phaedrus* and the *Symposium*, Virginia Woolf's reading matter in the 1920s, Plato not only qualifies his objection to poetry but emphasizes the *ekstasis* by which the lover of a beautiful person can transcend the fallacies of the world of sense-impressions to witness and become one with the Idea of Beauty itself:

What may we suppose to be the felicity of the man who sees absolute beauty in its essence, pure and unalloyed, who, instead of a beauty tainted by human flesh and colour and a mass of perishable rubbish, is able to apprehend divine beauty where it exists apart and alone? (*Symposium*, 212)

Mrs Ramsay's hypnotic and inexplicable beauty ravishes the senses and the spirit and has a mysterious property in that it inheres in a woman of fifty, well into middle age, drawing all eye-beams to itself and unifying the discrepant gazers: Charles Tansley, Mr Ramsay, Mr Bankes, Lily, Paul Rayley, and even, in a reluctant gesture of homage, Augustus Carmichael (p. 103). Lily's desperate desire to become 'like waters poured into one jar, inextricably the same, one with the object one adored' (p. 50) is so phrased as to imply, with its reiterated *one . . . one . . . one*, the Platonist home-sick longing to return to the One from which the soul splintered away into individual incarnation. Throughout the first Part of *To the Lighthouse*, Mrs Ramsay's beauty is interrogated: 'But was it nothing but looks? people said. What was there behind it – her beauty, her splendour?' (p. 31) The text supplies no answers to what 'people' query; it seems to know as little as any other observer what status to give Mrs Ramsay's beauty – whether to attribute its powerful unifying effects to the delusions of sense-impressions or to some greater meaning: earthly or heavenly beauty, the Platonist Venus Pandemos or Venus Urania. The 'rapture' or 'ecstasy' recurrently associated with the contemplation of her beauty are key-words in *To the Lighthouse*, and evidently drawn from the Greek *ekstasis* and Latin *raptus*, each one expressive of the seizure by force of the lover by the beauty of the beloved, the spirit's mystical initiation into an intuition of Plato's 'absolute beauty in its essence'. Such a state of mind abolishes the boundary between subject and object. Lily, both lover and artist, knows 'rapture' when 'losing consciousness of outer things' and when creativity arises in her 'like a fountain spurting' (p. 149), moving toward a state of 'illumination' (p. 150). An 'ecstacy' 'bursts' in Mrs

71

Ramsay's eyes and the universe seems to pour across the frontier between self and other, answering in transitory moments of visionary perception the troublesome questions raised by Plato's 'bed' and Mr Ramsay's 'table'.

The Platonist disgust with matter, that burial ground of the spirit, evidently confirmed an antipathy to the whole business of carnal and incarnate life in Time which deeply disturbed Virginia Woolf: the cramming of our mouths with fragments of dead creatures, the excretion of our own waste products, sexual coupling. Her life-records make clear the extent of her violent disaffinity with the flesh in which she was forced to reside. This Platonist aversion to 'the pollution of the walking sepulchre which we call a body, to which we are bound like an oyster to its shell' (*Phaedrus*, 250) is accompanied by incessant pangs of the equally familiar Platonist home-sickness, for that other pre-natal world of purity and rest – located by Virginia Woolf in the ocean, in the dead mother, in primal memory (life within the grape). The central Section of *To the Lighthouse* is a vision of the world minus mother. She cannot be found, and has taken all warmly human meaning with her. The world in her wake is a landscape composed of pure matter, words without signification, narrative *sans* story. The predominant image of a room nude of human occupation but dominated by a looking-glass fascinated Virginia Woolf. In *Jacob's Room*, a pair of old shoes keeps the shape of the dead young man's foot: 'What am I to do with these, Mr Bonamy?' (p. 168). What can be the use or meaning of the personal effects which record the eternal absence of the perishable child of Betty Flanders? Objects severed from their uses are represented by language drained of signification. Words become tokens of loss in this first of Virginia Woolf's great 'elegies':

> Listless is the air in an empty room, just swelling the curtain; the flowers in the jar shift. One fibre in the wicker armchair creaks, though no one sits there. (*Jacob's Room*, p. 168)

Such passages as this memorialize the calm, continuous state of shock in which a survivor witnesses the world as it remains when his friend or child has departed from it. Nothing has changed, but everything has changed. The empty room which has housed the living Jacob is the scene of his moment-by-moment absence, and contains other puzzling tokens of absence like the empty shoes and the empty chair which spectrally 'creaks' though no one sits there. Each item is a forum for an emptiness so inexplicable that the narrating observer obsessively studies it for clues to meaning, unable to reconcile himself to the godless, casual insignificance of a Jacobless reality. It was a fact of life which obsessively preoccupied Virginia Woolf and with which she never came to terms. In 1931, during the writing of the concluding pages of *The Waves*, her most experimental 'elegy' which moves as do *Jacob's Room* and *To the Lighthouse* around the loss of her brother Thoby (the prototype of Jacob and of Andrew Ramsay who explains to Lily about the 'table'), she noted in her diary that she had seen:

a silver & blue aeroplane in the middle of a field, apparently unhurt, among trees & cows. This morning the paper says three men were killed – the aeroplane dashing to the earth: But we went on, reminding me of that epitaph in the Greek anthology: when I sank, the other ships sailed on. (*Diary*, IV, p. 7)

What is important here and in the fictions is the role of the witness. Here, in their ignorance of the extremity that has come to pass in the field, the two witnesses pass by on their walk and have no sense of casualty until the morning paper reveals to them how little they knew of what they were seeing, a state of affairs germane to the novels which seek to map a universe of withheld secrets. That the scrap of epitaph she recollects should be both nautical and Greek also speaks volumes about the writer of *To the Lighthouse* and *The Waves*. The crashed Avro from Gatwick called to her mind Theodoridas's epitaph which runs, 'I am the tomb of a shipwrecked man; but set sail, stranger; for when we were lost, the other ships voyaged on' (Loeb, *Greek Anthology*, VII, 282). The poem records a bitter betrayal, the failure of man to interpose on behalf of man on the dangerous seas; and as Leonard and Virginia awaken the morning after the crash they have an uneasy sense of their treachery in strolling on their way, hearing 'the first spring birds: sharp egotistical'. So also *Jacob's Room*, *Mrs Dalloway* and *To the Lighthouse*, in witnessing the empty chair, the vacated shoes and the story of man that turns so soon to cheap anecdote and distorted hearsay, mediate in intense unease and distress the inexpiable guilt of the survivor.

The image of an uninhabited room dominated by a mirror came to be a central code not only for human perishability and dispensability but also for duplicity and guilt. In a short story of 1929, *The Lady in the Looking-Glass*, which owes something perhaps to the classicism of Wilde's novella, *The Picture of Dorian Gray*, the narrative persona is alone in an absent and inscrutable lady's room, using both the real room and the mirrored room to try to 'read' her character. In the 'real' room, there is mutability, the play of constant lights and shadows, as in Plato's Cave of the Senses, but the looking-glass world frames a crystallized version of this: 'all changing here, all stillness there' (*Complete Shorter Fiction*, p. 215). The persona, fabricating metaphors, imagines for the lady a 'fantastic ... tremulous' interior, like, say, a convolvulus (p. 216), but knows that the image-making facility simply interferes between the mind and the truth. Finally the lady enters the room and is annihilatingly disclosed by the cold fixity of the mirror as an unwholesomely 'naked' being, in whom 'there was nothing. Isabella was perfectly empty. She had no thoughts. She had no friends' (p. 219). The Platonist basis of the story is clear. In assessing the reality of any given object, we are directed away from our easily deluded eyesight, our equally fanciful imaginations, and toward the impersonal looking-glass which does not see with the eye of desire but is committed to an art of structural composition, transforming the objects of perception by a cold process of meaningful refraction:

Under the stress of thinking about Isabella, her room became more shadowy and symbolic; the corners seemed darker, the legs of chairs and tables more spindly and hieroglyphic. (*Complete Shorter Fiction*, p. 217)

Hieroglyphic chairs and tables write out the desires of the observer upon the *tabula rasa* of the material world. The story records the overwhelming need of the human observer that the world, properly read, should add up to a code of meaningful messages which would interest and comfort the reader. But the message of the cold-faced mirror is that the universe is in itself quite meaningless, an assemblage of shapes and surfaces where we throw out desire's images like a film upon a screen, signifying however (when we withdraw our luminous gazes and picture the chair or table in our own absence as if with looking-glass vision) nothing whatsoever. If by the mirror the story means 'art', this is an art which sees with terrible, ruthless eye. The sharp *peripeteia* reveals a state of things which Virginia Woolf most feared: the absurdity of life without a self; ontological draining, the equivalent of Forster's 'panic and emptiness' (*Howard's End*, p. 33), the 'Boum' in the Marabar Caves (*A Passage to India*, p. 145). The atmosphere generated is a kind of boredom and inertia, as in deep depression, Boredom raised to a metaphysical response to a world reduced to mere materiality.

The central section of *To the Lighthouse* converts the horror of this emptiness into a vision of Apocalypse at the death of meaning. A cold, sardonic tone that varies between rapturous disrelish and dead-eyed shock chronicles the exposure of the relinquished room to the unblinking stare of the mirror:

Now, day after day, light turned, like a flower reflected in water, its clear image on the wall opposite. Only the shadows of the trees, flourishing in the wind, made obeisance on the wall, and for a moment darkened the pool in which light reflected itself; or birds, flying, made a soft spot flutter slowly across the bedroom floor.

So loveliness reigned and stillness, and together made the shape of loveliness itself, a form from which life had parted; solitary like a pool at evening, far distant, seen from a train window, vanishing so quickly that the pool, pale in the evening, is scarcely robbed of its solitude, though once seen. Loveliness and stillness clasped hands in the bedroom, and among the shrouded jugs and sheeted chairs even the prying of the wind, and the soft nose of the clammy sea airs, rubbing, snuffling, iterating, and reiterating their questions – 'Will you fade? Will you perish?' – scarcely disturbed the peace, the indifference, the air of pure integrity, as if the question they asked scarcely needed that they should answer: we remain. (pp. 120–1)

The revolutionary central Section invades with words the realm of the tonguelessly inanimate; attributes intentionality to the insentient (the vagrant 'airs' which trespass ruinously upon the domestic interior) and hence supplies 'plot' to passive recrudescence; dignifies a blank instrument of reflection, the mirror, with the status of a visionary witness. A new twist is given to art's 'holding the mirror up to nature': the mirror has a purity unknown to the human eye. It gives back only what confronts it, no more and no less. It neither criticizes nor desires the object of perception, for it can neither love nor hate. The emotion generated in this Section resembles that of a *danse macabre*, the horror of the rape of the sanctuary of meaning established in Part One being increased by the congratulatory mood with which the text welcomes the mirror-vision. The dehumanization of the inner world is greeted with terrible composure as the author assimilates the looking-glass world in the empty house to the world of the Platonic Forms or Ideas. The mirror opposes the lighthouse (signifying insight, mediation, eyes with a spirit – a guide, signal and benignly beaconing messenger) by representing the seeing Eye with no mind behind it. In the absence of love, there is only the narcissism connoted by the mirror: the sterile self-adoration of Narcissus entranced with his own image in the pool ('like a flower reflected in water'). The mirror's cold receptivity withholds interpretation of the cyclical light dappled with shadows which the sun daily casts upon the opposite wall. This system of meaningless reflections is very close to the Platonic conception of a concatenation of *Un*realities – the mere *shadows* of *images* in a *pool*, all Platonist counters for our chronic state of delusion in the material world. Virginia Woolf is working here in a language into which Neoplatonism had hundreds of years earlier invoked the Narcissus *topos* as an emblem of vain perception:

The young Narcissus, that is the soul of rash and inexperienced man, does not look at his own face, does not notice his own proper substance and qualities, but pursues his shadow in water and tries to embrace it, that is he admires beauty in a fragile body and in running water, which is a shadow of the mind itself, and turns his back on his own beauty.

... And so he dissolves into tears and is destroyed ... (Ficino, *Commentary on Plato's Symposium, Renaissance Views of Man*, p. 50)

Yet the Platonism in Virginia Woolf's passage is twofold and duplicitous. For the house free of human use is also with insidious irony mediated as a place of 'pure integrity', in which the Platonic Forms reveal themselves and unite before the mindless mirror. Amongst the 'shrouds' of the sheeted furniture, in this morgue of human pretension and affectation, Light (the Platonic sign for Reality) reflects itself. The narrative eye gets in as insidiously as the intrusive airs through the keyhole of fiction to bear witness to what no human eye *can*, in reality, witness: things-in-themselves, pure of human consciousness (*Think of a table ... when you aren't there*). Words summon the wordless; an imagistic style displays the unseen. The 'loveliness' and 'stillness' that marry into 'the shape of loveliness itself, a form', explicitly evoke Plato's Form or Idea of Beauty, the abstract essence which is 'absolute, existing alone with itself, unique, eternal' (*Symposium*, 211a). The onanistic character of this inhuman world in which the Narcissus emblem (the sterile self-involvement of the world we live in) predominates carries a sinister threat. For if the emptied house is Narcissus, then the narrative voice is Echo, the rejected nymph dying to a bodiless voice in the cave of unmeaning.

Virginia Woolf had a deep-rooted horror of mirrors which affects the whole mood of the central Section of *To the Lighthouse*. In *A Sketch of the Past*, she recounts and investigates the sources of this repulsion:

There was a small looking-glass in the hall at Talland House. It had, I remember, a ledge with a brush on it. By standing on tiptoe I could see my face in the glass. When I was six or seven perhaps, I got into the habit of looking at my face in the glass. But I only did this if I was sure that I was alone. I was ashamed of it. A strong feeling of guilt seemed naturally attached to it ... I must have been ashamed or afraid of my own body. Another memory, also of the hall, may help to explain this. There was a slab outside the dining room door for standing dishes upon. Once when I was very small Gerald Duckworth lifted me onto this, and as I sat there he began to explore my body.

... I dreamt that I was looking in a glass when a horrible face – the face of an animal – suddenly showed over my shoulder. I cannot be sure if this was a dream, or if it happened. (pp. 78–80)

In the midst of her Paradise at St Ives loomed the lidless eye of the mirror in the hall. The mirror was always there as she passed through the corridor between rooms, and reflected her body whether she looked into it or not. Confronting her fascinating reflection, she boiled with shame; yet wanted to do it. Once there appeared a monster in the mirror, which was a manifestation of her self. The anguish of sexual horror also seems to linger throughout 'Time Passes'. The evacuated house consecrates the nuptials of ghosts – 'Loveliness and stillness *clasped hands*' amongst the sheeted furniture (my emphasis added) – in place of the warmly human union of Mr and Mrs Ramsay. The incursion of floods of darkness into the house (a *jeu d'esprit* which owes so much technically to Dickens's method with fog in *Bleak House* and with winds in *Our Mutual Friend*) and the maleficent 'airs' which, invisible but tactile, gate-crash the desecrated sanctum (pp. 117–18) like unbidden guests which 'nose' and 'fumble' the contours of sleepers and household objects, have a sinister sexual connotation. These windy spirits, like menacing, pointless Ariels, are obscenely inquisitive presences, turning the act of witnessing (the narrator's proper function) to a salacious voyeurism. The verbs associated with them express unwelcome, unacknowledged touching, of an illicit nature. The author puts her characters to sleep in the second Section of Part Two, and lays them open to the investigations of these 'airs' which *nose, fumble, rub* the sleeping household. There is a sense of sexual curiosity, the penetration of the inside by the outside, as the sleepers impersonate the damned in Dante, void of personality as they sleep, open to the erasing flood-tides of darkness which blot them out. Like the inhabitants of a madhouse their behaviour is non-purposive: 'Sometimes a hand was raised as if to clutch something or ward off something' (p. 117). The text images the hand as severed as it responds to the bad dream. Limbs twitch; mouths laugh meaninglessly and the narrative takes down at dictation an account of relationlessness and absurdity, as the Flood

77

rots the Ark. The house, like a brain-washed mind, is taken over by vagrant elements and taught to seek its own destruction. In the 'shut eyes and the loosely clasping fingers' there is a suggestion of the spellbound Briar Rose story in which the whole castle is entranced and will not awaken for a hundred years: catatonic sexual terror seems to reside both in the imagery and in the manner in which it is related. Virginia Woolf (writing with hectic speed, as the Diary testifies) is telling the worst she has ever suspected or dreamt about the world. The strange, collusive joy which animates the tone is perhaps aptly compared with the awry emotion that can be generated by great shock. In her diary entry for 5 May, 1924, she had described something of that deranging incongruity between the experience and its expression:

This is the 29th anniversary of mothers death. I think it happened early on a Sunday morning, & I looked out of the nursery window & saw old Dr Seton walking away with his hands behind his back, as if to say It is finished, & then the doves descending, to peck in the road, I suppose, with a fall & descent of inifinite peace. I was 13, & could fill a whole page & more with my impressions of that day, many of them ill received by me, & hidden from the grown ups, but very memorable on that account: how I laughed, for instance, behind the hand which was meant to hide my tears; & through the fingers saw the nurses sobbing. (*Diary*, II, pp. 300–1)

Her memoir, *A Sketch of the Past*, endorses this, and adds a looking-glass in the room containing her mother's death-bed:

At any rate I remember the long looking-glass; with the drawers on either side; and the washstand; and the great bed on which my mother lay. I remember very clearly how even as I was taken to the bedside I noticed that one nurse was sobbing, and a desire to laugh came over me, and I said to myself as I have often done at moments of crisis since, 'I feel nothing whatever'. Then I stooped and kissed my mother's face. It was still warm. She [had] only died a moment before. (*Moments of Being*, pp. 106–7)

The tone of the central Section of *To the Lighthouse* impersonates both the hysteria of traumatizing shock that laughs at agony too estranging for tears, with their remedial sensible balm, and the anaesthesia recorded in the memoir and shared with the shell-shocked Septimus Warren Smith in *Mrs Dalloway* whose most crucifying stigma is 'the panic ... that he could not feel' (p. 96). Alienated from its own emotion, the self is completely lost: it has walked out from the body of the sufferer, vacated it like a derelict house and stepped, perhaps, into the mirror where it takes on, like a nightmarish Alice, a separate and entirely meaningless existence. The mirror recorded in her mother's death-room is another sign for Virginia Woolf of Septimus's unatonable knowledge: 'it might be possible that the world itself is without meaning' (p. 98). 'Time Passes', with its modulations between the chilling semblance of narrative indifference, apocalyptic frenzy, gentle elegy, lyricism turned up to full volume and vatic oratory, can be imagined as that part of *To the Lighthouse* which might have been composed by Septimus Warren Smith.

The third Section of 'Time Passes' deals with Apocalypse and concludes in the parenthetical death of Mrs Ramsay. The pace accelerates as in speeded film, and the prose orchestrates crashing chords of mighty literary, religious and historical allusion:

The autumn trees, ravaged as they are, take on the flash of tattered flags kindling in the gloom of cool cathedral caves where gold letters on marble pages describe death in battle ... (p. 119)

There is a complex development of imagery from the visual gold that is the relic of the year's growth on the trees, and remembers Shakespeare's 'yellow leaves, or none, or few' of the *Sonnets* (LXXIII) so important in Part One and the epic vision of the dead or damned as fallen leaves of autumn: Virgil's 'multitudinous as the leaves of the forest that in the first frost fall away and drop' (*Aeneid*, VI, 309–10); Dante's 'As, in the autumn, leaves detach themselves ...' (*Inferno*, III, 112); Milton's 'Thick as autumnal leaves that strow the brooks/In Vallombrosa' *Paradise Lost*, I, 302–3). The remnant of leaves on the bough is assimilated to military banners in the dark interior of a cathedral commemorating the battalions of the honoured dead: gold leaves, gold banners, gold letters of the epitaphs of the legions who have fallen in played-out battles, on a marmoreal scroll of honour. Virginia Woolf closes the book of life and opens the Book of Death with its unturnable marble pages. Pierced by the 'kindling' of flags high in the vaulted darkness of the imagined cathedral, the sanctuary of the fathers – the church militant – testifies to its 'victories'. This is the first intimation of the World War which underlies the central panel of the novel's tryptych. With its huge drumroll of alliteration and assonance – *cool cathedral caves, battle ... bones bleach ... burn, flash ... flags* – the prose satirizes the music of martial splendour and assimilates the death-dealing armies of the patriarchal world to the blind, sad brutalities of the state of nature. *To the Lighthouse* takes as a major topic, all the more effective for being phrased in the minor key, Wilfred Owen's focus:

'War and the pity of War'. It displaces the idea of heroism and rebukes the male idea of honour by assigning to female labours an Homeric status. Female activities, traditionally derided by the ruling culture as menial, are celebrated as acts of creation, sustaining the fabric of things: activities with the broom, mop and scrubbing brush exemplified in Mrs McNab; Mrs Ramsay's cutting of Mr Ramsay's hair into a pudding basin; the care of children; most especially the activities of sewing or knitting. In *Mrs Dalloway*, Lucrezia sews a hat. And somehow that simple workmanship (which is also a state of mind, comparable perhaps to the quiet absorption and peacefulness we share when we look at a Dutch picture like Vermeer's *The Lace Maker*) opposes for the lacerated, wrung mind of the shell-shocked Septimus the desecration of his war experience. It stands for sanity, patience, creation: 'She built it up; first one thing, then another, she built it up, sewing' (p. 161):

She was a flowering tree; and through her branches looked out the face of a lawgiver, who had reached a sanctuary where she feared no one... (*Mrs Dalloway*, pp. 163–4)

Woman creates; man uncreates. In *To the Lighthouse*, Mrs Ramsay's knitting of the stocking as a gesture of fellowship for the lighthouse-keeper's son has the same timeless, mythic quality of one who is, though engaged in homely work accounted trivial, 'a flowering tree', 'a lawgiver', raising the values embodied on the 'distaff side' to a power resembling those of the Fates, the measuring, spinning and cutting of the threads of life – but, in so far as it is given to human nature to be so, benign and sheltering rather than (as in the case of the Fates) cruelly arbitrary. The central Part of *To the Lighthouse* exposes, however, the fact that the 'lawgiver', arbiter of sanity and redefiner of male 'honour' as female wisdom and mercy is in bondage: to Time, war and mortality. Her name is first in Part Two's roll-call of the dead. The sonorous, sermonical voice which questions 'divine goodness' in the third Section, echoes St John of Patmos in its revelation of the portents of war, pestilence, natural calamity and the arising of the beast out of the sea (*Revelation* 13: 1–4). 'For the great day of his wrath is come; and who shall be able to stand?' (6: 17).

But alas, divine goodness, twitching the cord, draws the curtain; it does not please him; he covers his treasures in a drench of hail, and so breaks them, so confuses them that it seems impossible that their calm should ever return or that we should ever compose from their fragments a perfect whole or read in the littered pieces the clear words of truth. For our penitence deserves a glimpse only; our toil respite only.

    The nights now are full of wind and destruction; the trees plunge and bend and their leaves fly helter skelter until the lawn is plastered with them and they lie packed in gutters and choke rain pipes and scatter damp paths. (p. 119)

A multitude of allusions crowd behind Virginia Woolf's text here like mighty ghosts testifying to the end of the world: first amongst them is St John's vision of the Last Things (Heaven, Hell, Death and Judgement), but there is also Pope's *Apocalypse* ('Thy hand, great Anarch, lets the curtain fall . . .' [see p. 30]) and Tennyson's:

> To-night the winds begin to rise
>   And roar from yonder dropping day;
>   The last red leaf is whirl'd away,
> The rooks are blown about the skies;
>
> The forest crack'd, the waters curl'd . . .
>   (*In Memoriam*, XV)

The scattering of the leaves in a litter of confusion recalls and extends the novel's assimilation of the leaves of vegetation to the leaves of a book. The outside world is a system of blank pages on which the characters imaginatively inscribe and record their personal beliefs and insights in a fashion which stabilizes the individual in the matrix of being, and helps him to feel at home there. In Part One, Mr Ramsay toured the garden, deep in thought. His peripatetic progress is recorded as a habitual journey round a series of mental landmarks:

He slipped seeing before him that hedge which had over and over again rounded some pause, signified some conclusion, seeing his wife and child, seeing again the urns with the trailing red geraniums which had so often decorated processes of thought, and bore, written up among their leaves, as if they were scraps of paper on which one scribbles notes in the rush of reading – he slipped, seeing all this, smoothly into speculation . . . (p. 43)

The hedge, his wife and child, the urns with the geraniums are all accorded palimpsestic significance; they are a private code which relates in a specific pattern of meaningfulness for Mr Ramsay, rather as Lily's arrangement of the salt cellar in relation to the pattern on the table-cloth is her shorthand for the composition of her picture, and the pear tree is the site of the imaginary table which signifies her perception of Mr Ramsay's profession. The philosopher perambulates the contents of his own mind, using the external world as a collection of manuscript on which he has written out his mental conjurations, as memoranda. Walking and thinking are focused as one and the same activity, as they were for both Virginia Woolf and her father. Geranium leaves (which for Mrs Ramsay are just geranium leaves, and beautiful) exist for Mr Ramsay as the stock not of the garden but of the mind. The narrator's word-play converts them to leaves of paper covered in a scribbled mnemonic, according to that system of coding whereby we hang out thoughts on bushes and reflect them in the sky. The world is made intelligible not by the perceiver's submission to what it is in itself (which is finally unknowable) but by the system of meanings in which he drapes what he sees. The passage intimates a kind of Sibylline authority fragmented and split upon the phenomena of the external world, and attributes to the questing mind a kind of combination of cartography and calligraphy as it 'reads' the problems of 'subject and object and the nature of reality' and 'writes out' its speculations and solutions upon the Book of Nature. For each of us in our own garden, the world is comfortingly covered with specimens of our own hand-writing. Part Two of *To the Lighthouse* exposes the oracular garden to the 'wind and destruction' of autumn. The leaves of the trees are whipped away from their source and inextricably muddled; the leaves of the corporate testament of the family who have written their own reality upon their surroundings are disbound and 'littered' through the garden in a sodden mass of confusion, recalling the torn-up letters in the waste-paper basket of Section 2 (p. 118). The narrative voice now introduces an anonymous 'sleeper' who keeps vigil at the sea-shore, asking the unanswerable questions, in the absence of Mr Ramsay who also walked to the very edge of his garden (the locus of language and meaning) and quested at the insecure shore-line for Truth. The 'sleeper' is kept awake throughout the central Part, to act as a chorus for humanity pursuing its humanistic dream of a world which should 'reflect the compass of the soul' in the face of the terrible evidence against such faith amassed by the narrator. It is this section that concludes in the parenthetical death of Mrs Ramsay and the breaking of the conjugal unit:

[Mr Ramsay stumbling along a passage stretched his arms out one dark morning, but, Mrs Ramsay having died rather suddenly the night before, he stretched his arms out. They remained empty.] (p. 120)

Again there is remembrance of Tennyson and *In Memoriam*:

Tears of the widower, when he sees
  A late-lost form that sleep reveals,
  And moves his doubtful arms, and feels
Her place is empty, fall like these.

(XIII)

Empty arms, an empty place in a bed, empty house, empty '. . . shoes, a shooting cap, some faded skirts and coats in wardrobes' (p. 120): the widower, the house with its sheddings of obsolete clothing that holds the beloved shape, become like reliquaries, matter drained of spirit. The parenthetical casualty report shocks readers by its deadpan brevity, one might say the *emptiness* of its manner: Mrs Ramsay dies not only in parenthesis and offstage as in Greek drama, but (as in the later accounts of Prue's and Andrew's deaths [pp. 123,124]) irrelevantly. We are reminded of the daily wartime newspaper lists of death in battle, the unreadably infinite scroll of names of those who died *for King and Country*, or, as the text of *To the Lighthouse* implies, for nothing at all, for empty words. In a world where life and language were so cheap and a political world in which 'The necessary supply of heroes to the Western Front must be maintained at all costs' (Carson), one civilian death can be of no possible moment. Besides the anaesthesia of shock so ably suggested by the text's failure or refusal to respond emotionally to the deaths it memorializes, these off-centre, off-key reports of tragedies germane to the novel and yet represented as digressive to the narcissistic brooding of the house upon its own interior manage to imply a universal human impairment during the war years, and to expose 'the old Lie: *Dulce et decorum est*/*Pro patria mori*' (Wilfred Owen, *Dulce et decorum*, lines 27–8). In the waste land of 'Time Passes' the mother perishes not only in parenthesis but in a subordinate clause and *rather* suddenly, a sardonic invocation of the trivialization of catastrophe in gossip, 'Mrs Ramsay is dead you know – yes, she died rather suddenly.'

The death of Mrs Ramsay is registered as the passing of Beauty, that of Prue and Andrew as the passing of Youth. It is important to recognize the universal status accorded to these persons in Part Two in order to acknowledge the vastness of the issues to which it is addressed. In *A Sketch of the Past*, Virginia Woolf meditates upon her mother's 'astonishing beauty':

Perhaps I never became conscious of it; I think I accepted her beauty as the natural quality that a mother – she seemed typical, universal, yet our own in

83

particular – had by virtue of being our mother. It was part of her calling. I do not think I separated her face from that general being; or from her whole body. (p. 95)

This passage corresponds to a quality we recognize in *To the Lighthouse* of Mrs Ramsay's indelible beauty as assimilated to her maternal solicitude. Indeed, she appears in the tenth Section of 'The Window', for all her faults, as an emblem of maternal love, bringing to mind the old personification of Charity as a nursing mother, offering the breast to a crowd of clamorous infants, as in Spenser's Charissa ('A multitude of babes about her hong,/Playing their sports, that ioyed her to behold,/Whom still she fed . . .' *Faerie Queene*, I. x. 31):

Why, she asked, pressing her chin on James's head, should they grow up so fast? Why should they go to school? She would have liked always to have had a baby. She was happiest carrying one in her arms. Then people might say she was tyrannical, domineering, masterful, if they chose; she did not mind. And, touching his hair with her lips, she thought, he will never be so happy again . . . (p. 57)

As an icon of maternity, Mrs Ramsay is almost always seen in the context of children, in beatitudinous relationship with James as she watches him cutting out the picture of a refrigerator on the first page, measuring him for a sock, reading to him, telling bedtime tales to Cam, watching Prue and Jasper throwing catches, letting Rose choose her jewels, thinking how a tenpenny teaset made Cam happy for days, mothering her house-guests. Beauty in *To the Lighthouse* is part of this 'calling'. The death of Mrs Ramsay is the withdrawal of the love-source from the world of the novel, leaving in its wake a universe that is an empty frame, like Lily's picture, awaiting its subject. Even with the reconstruction of a livable world in Part Three, the vacuity at the centre of the bereaved post-war generation's experience remains. It is known to Lily as to no other character because as an artist it is her task to fill the representation of that space with meaningful form:

Suddenly, the empty drawing-room steps, the frill of the chair inside, the puppy tumbling on the terrace, the whole wave and whisper of the garden became like curves and arabesques flourishing round a centre of complete emptiness. (p. 166)

This sentence, with its immaculate precision and poise (*wave and whisper/curves and arabesques*) is one of the finest verbal Impressionist miniatures Virginia Woolf ever constructed. The garden becomes a dream-world, or looking-glass world without the mirror, conveying an unaccountable Alice-in-Wonderland strangeness and threat. This is the same garden whose every leaf was a meaningful mnemonic for Mr Ramsay in Part One, keeping green his round of thoughts; whose lawn was 'plastered' with these same leaves in Part Two, divorced from signification; which now in Part Three composes itself with bland preciosity into a soft-voiced new message, whispering and gesturing to the observer about nothing at all. In the looking-glass garden, the spirit Romanticism saw as uniting 'All thinking things, all objects of all thought' that 'rolls through all things' (Wordsworth, *Tintern Abbey*, 102, 103) or Christians view as an indwelling presence in the material universe, is perfectly, purely absent. The picture that solicits Lily's eye has unity but no spirit. At its centre is an absurdity more chilling because less ambiguous than the hyacinth garden experience in Eliot's *The Waste Land*: 'I knew nothing,/Looking into the heart of light, the silence' (I. 39–40). The sentence consciously stylizes its pictorial elements in a threefold elaboration (steps, the chair-frill, the puppy), moving to synthesis of relationships in the 'whole' composition. Objects are formalized as decorative features: the detail of the frill, for instance, insists on aesthetic values extraneous to utility. The design of the garden is interpreted in the second half of the sentence as replete with insinuation – 'waves' of greeting, 'whisper[ed]' suggestive messages, reminiscent of the talking trees and expository birds which relate to Septimus in *Mrs Dalloway* disabling intimations from eternity. The 'arabesques' of the garden which motion as preciously as classical ballet, and the 'flourishing' greenery which connotes luxuriant growth and repeats the balletic stylization with a flamboyance of gesture like that of an Elizabethan signature, represent a picture of an empty frame, an ornate and mannered organization of decorative effects as in passe-partout, directing the eye into the centre of the picture: the centre of self, or world, or literary artefact which contains nothing at all. It is as if, for a moment, Lily's eye is glazed into a mirror and receives a traumatizing mirror's-eye-view of the world minus her heart's desire: landscape without a figure, background in search of foreground.

In Western art, centrality has by tradition supplied the focus of meaning. *To the Lighthouse* is a three-part structure, in which Part Two, the centre, both calls attention to itself as in the central panel of a tyrptych on which the outer panels comment, and as a mediating section, as in the second movement of a three-movement symphony or concerto which links the themes in the first and third movements. The novel, like Lily's picture, gestures toward its own 'centre of emptiness', making all that is seen (through 'The Window') and sought (The

Lighthouse') dependent on the mortal 'Time Passes'. In Passion tryp-tyches, the central panel represents the crucifixion itself. So too in *To the Lighthouse*, the central Section enacts a ritualized, unatoning sacrifice of the precious sacred places and presiding figure of Part One; the hearth and household gods are sacked and the enactments of the first and third Parts deeply questioned. The Modernistic use of centrality lies in the novel's identification of the centre as empty of meaning: a hole in the continuum which the pen-stroke of the author, like the brush-strokes of Lily, are hoveringly uncertain how to fill. The terror of this central void is articulated in the minor key throughout the work, most profoundly in Lily's long-term debate with herself as to what is wanted to harmonize her picture. The salt cellar on a flower in the pattern of the table cloth at the dinner party becomes a memo to 'put the tree further in the middle; then I shall avoid that awkward space' (p. 80). Ten years later, completing the picture, covering for the destabilizing absence of her sitter, Lily can only finish, and put up her brushes, when she has found a way to fill the agonizing centre: 'With a sudden intensity, as if she saw it clear for a second, she drew a line there, in the centre. It was done; it was finished' (p. 192). At this point also Virginia Woolf is preparing to finish *To the Lighthouse*: two voices, Lily's and Virginia's, seem to speak to us in unison as the narrative prepares to close. It is perhaps one of the author's most scintillating pieces of *trompe-l'oeil*, to delude us into thinking that she too can 'draw a line there, in the centre'. For what the visual artist is free to do, her art working in the medium of simultaneity, the literary artist cannot effect. She works in Time and her pen can never return to the empty centre to fill its emptiness and substitute a voice for its echo.

'How could any Lord have made this world?' Mrs Ramsay inquired of herself in the first Part. She turned the lighthouse beam of her inner integrity upon the godless suffering of the creaturely world and her soul's rigour could not affirm any divine meaning in the pattern (p. 62). Her works of charity represent her defiance of that régime in which there 'is no reason, order, justice: but suffering, death, the poor'. Her stern isolation as she acknowledges the moral void at the heart of the creation intimidates and awes her lugubrious husband on patrol so that he swerves and will not visit his moans upon her. Part Two exposes the truth of her insight, fulfilling the prophecies intimated by her severe expression. And yet she has had a twofold function: to know, and to protect the eyes of the young from this hope-quenching knowledge. As mediatrix and guardian of eyesight, Mrs Ramsay mantles or cloaks reality, meting it out in a fashion she conceives her brood can tolerate. Her first words, the first speech in the book, represent her in this counterpaning activity, saying *Yes* to James's hope of visiting the lighthouse, with only a soft conditional: *if it's fine to-morrow* (p. 9). As she leaves the house to join her husband and children in the garden, she takes a green shawl from the picture frame and folds it around her shoulders (p. 63). Just as every work of literature teaches its attentive reader from Page One the reading-method appropriate to itself, so *To the Lighthouse* has taught its reader to take account of symbols and symbolic patterns of recurrence in the smallest of details as perhaps the most important generators of meaning in the work. This way of reading becomes automatic for the novel. The wonderful strangeness of the transformative powers of Virginia Woolf's language is finely caught by Lily's feeling that the snatches of poetry so madly emitted by Mr Ramsay as he strides around take extrinsic form: 'the words became symbols, wrote themselves all over the grey-green walls' (p. 138). Even within this apparently literal fragment of a sentence, the principle Lily notes is covertly operating. For the text need not have specified *grey-green* walls; any colour or no colour would have done. By colouring the walls, the narrative voice not only adds the sense of immediacy of location to the thought process but links this moment back into the complex and subtle colour-coding system which has been established by the stress placed on colour in specific contexts throughout Part One. Green and grey are Mrs Ramsay's colours, green for her life, grey for her death. The green cloak shares the virtue of the whole chlorophyll-based creation: it is the lawn which mantles the underworld and its mysteries of seed and grave, sentience without predatoriness, the bringing-forth and nurturing of children. Standing in the garden under the failing light, to wear the green cloak is to be part of the garden; to stand with her children's father watching her children makes the two of them 'symbolical ... representative ... in the dusk standing, looking, the symbols of marriage, husband and wife' (p. 69). The grey cloak comes into its own posthumously. It is Mrs Ramsay's gardening cloak, Mrs NcNab recalls as she fingers it in the eighth Section of Part Two and visualizes the dead woman with a child, in her garden stooping over her flowers (p. 126). To wear the grey cloak is to become a wraith or ghost, an emanation from the unreal world superimposed by the mind upon the world-without-her. Mrs NcNab both conjures and fails to conjure her by hypnotic repetition: 'There was the old grey cloak ... she could see her ... in that grey cloak ... She could see her now ...

faint and flickering, like a yellow beam or the circle at the end of a telescope, a lady in a grey cloak' (pp. 126–7). The text calls her up unreally, a spectral image one might walk through. *To the Lighthouse* not only structures itself on symbolic patternings, it also turns an intelligent, querying eye upon its own processes. Just as it exploits language to question the authority of language (see pp. 61 ff.), so it investigates the function of symbolism in human perception, reflecting upon the way the symbol mediates the inveterate antagonism between things-as-they-are and things-as-we-wish-them-to-be, doing justice to each of these irreconcilables. Like Mrs Ramsay's green cloak over the death's head in the children's bedroom, it both covers reality by counterfeiting for it and signals the underlying reality by demarcating it. The symbol therefore stands midway between Lily's conundrum of 'subject and object' providing a subtle lens by careful use of which the perceiver may attempt to make his peace with reality. When Lily's mind throws out words as symbols over the 'grey-green wall', she goes on to think, 'If only she could put them together . . . write them out in some sentence, then she would have got at the truth of things' (p. 138). This complete verbal mimesis of the writing on the wall is the aim and object of the novel itself.

The novel is a sustained act of transformation, representing, like an alchemical experiment, a threefold psychic process from creation, through dissolution to reconstruction. In each phase of the spiritual action, it is the symbols which transform under adjusted and readjusted lights and perspectives. At the beginning of the novel, the lighthouse, the focal symbol according to which all other symbols and events are read, is uniformly far distant; at the end, the quest achieved, it is close at hand: 'So that was the Lighthouse, was it? No, the other was also the Lighthouse. For nothing was simply one thing' (p. 172). Originally, it is perceived as light; ultimately as house, a modulation which extends the scope of our double vision by re-addressing us to the beginning in the end. The threefold structure here acts as a classic progression of thesis, antithesis, synthesis. The mediating symbol of the green cloak also undergoes transformation over the course of the novel, its magical and talismanic properties being tested out against the mortality it was meant to cover, in Part Two. Two events disturb the plotless plot which covers for the stasis in the Platonic hall of mirrors of the abandoned house:

Once only a board sprang on the landing; once in the middle of the night with a roar, with a rupture, as after centuries of quiescence, a rock rends itself from the mountain and hurtles crashing into the valley, one fold of the shawl loosened and swung to and fro. (p. 121)

But in the very lull of this loving caress, as the long stroke leant upon the bed, the rock was rent asunder; another fold of the shawl loosened; there it hung, and swayed . . .

But . . . there came later in the summer ominous sounds like the measured blows of hammers dulled on felt, which, with their repeated shocks still further loosened the shawl and cracked the tea-cups. (p. 124)

Why, it was all damp in here; the plaster was falling. Whatever did they want to hang a beast's skull there for? gone mouldy too. (p. 127)

Mrs Bast . . . wondered, putting her cup down, whatever they hung that beast's skull there for? Shot in foreign parts no doubt. (p. 130)

If, as many cultures believe and it is hard for the bereaved entirely to rule out of possibility, the dead leave behind them echoes or vestiges of their living power, then Mrs Ramsay's vestige is the cloak, whose function it is in the second Part to fall away, and fail in its mediatorial mission to deny the thing it covers, whilst preserving it *in situ*. We feel that Mrs Ramsay's maternal power survives indwelling in the relic; that, while the cloak remains, her spirit has not truly passed from the house; and that the apparently insignificant article of clothing distinguishes itself from the pathos of untenanted gloves, hats, dresses – those material trivia which return at once to matter, the moment the possessor abandons them – by retaining its use, and hence its symbolic meaning. The use of the cloak is to intervene between the unwilling eyes and the *memento mori*: it saves the only human witnesses of the scene – the narrator and the reader – from direct contemplation of the terror beneath. Its failure yields up the skull beneath to the spectral eye of the mirror.

Mrs Ramsay's cloak is the female and maternal equivalent of Prospero's rod, his 'art' in *The Tempest*. With this art, he redirects the stories of the characters on his island, providing an ultimately benign and redressing magic of paternal rebuke and reaffiliation: but with Act V, the potency of the 'rough magic' (i. 50) is reaching its terminus and 'Every third thought shall be my grave' (V. i. 311). Mrs Ramsay's 'art' survives her death, far from her island realm where she reigned as 'queen' (p. 77) and officiated as high-priestess (p. 94), by a little. The gradual fall charted in the apocalyptic Part Two has reverberations in terms of every kind of spiritual issue the novel touches. As it falls, it is paradoxically raised to epic and mythic status. In the first allusion quoted above, the loosening of one fold is compared, in an epic simile, with the violence and shock of a rockfall on a mountain side, centuries in the making, a grotesquely disproportionate but brilliantly apposite similitude in terms of the total lack of immediate causation in the deathly still house, with the stealthy gathering of invisible impetus in a destructive act of monumental consequence. In the second allusion, as another fold loosens, the 'long stroke' of the lighthouse beam (identified whimsically by Mrs Ramsay as 'her stroke . . . her own eyes meeting her own eyes' [p. 61]) is syntactically angled to make it appear as the cause that 'the rock was rent asunder' and another fold loosened. This represents a major transformation of the symbolic cloak within a matrix of expanding symbolisms. The epic rockfall assumes a cosmic spiritual significance by assimilation to the Scriptural account of Christ's atonement. The shawl takes on the aspect of the veil of the Temple when Christ gave up the ghost, and looks simultaneously back to Mrs Ramsay's premonitory 'It will end, It will end' (p. 61), across to the narrative voice's 'it was finished' (p. 131) in relation to the house's restoration, and forward to Lily's 'It was done; it was finished' (p. 192). *Consummatum est* is a requiem, a sacrifice and an atonement.

And, behold, the veil of the temple was rent in twain from the top to the bottom; and the earth did quake, and the rocks rent;

And the graves were opened; and many bodies of the saints which slept arose (*Matthew* 27:51–2)

Matthew's 'the rocks rent' is repeated in Virginia Woolf's 'the rock was rent asunder', raising the language to a Biblical register of authority in alluding to the earthquake which terrified the Israelites into acknowledging Christ as the Son of God. The desecration of the sanctum portends the Day of Judgment, the earthquake being a sign of God's implacable ire with man. These earthquake suggestions are perpetuated as the 'hammer-blows' from the trenches in France which further disturb the cloak, culminating in the casualty report on Andrew Ramsay with all its chillingly business-like brevity and the official gloss of his mercifully instantaneous death (p. 124). We do not see the cloak fall. The exposed skull is disclosed as a conversation-piece for Mrs Bast and Mrs McNab, as little able to terrify their immune commonsense as someone else's nightmare told in broad daylight.

When Mrs Ramsay covered the distressing skull from Cam's eyes in Part One, she cloaked it not only in her green mantle but in her storyteller's art. In dislodging the covering from the underlying reality, the narrator of Part Two reveals the white lie or well-intended cheat at the heart of the mother's bedtime stories to her children. Virginia Woolf's story is of a self-consciously different order, exposing the cover-up of lovely, lulling fictions through the medium of a fiction for insomniac readers. Faced with the dilemma of her boy-child's passionate compulsion to retain the pig's head on the wall and her girl-child's repugnance, Mrs Ramsay's solution is a makeshift compromise:

> she quickly took her own shawl off and wound it round the skull, round and round and round, and then she came back to Cam and laid her head almost flat on the pillow beside Cam's and said how lovely it looked now; how the fairies would love it; it was like a bird's nest; it was like a beautiful mountain such as she had seen abroad, with valleys and flowers and bells ringing and birds singing and little goats and antelopes . . . She could see the words echoing as she spoke them rhythmically in Cam's mind, and Cam was repeating after her how it was like a mountain, a bird's nest, a garden, and there were little antelopes, and her eyes were opening and shutting, and Mrs Ramsay went on saying still more monotonously, and more rhythmically and more nonsensically, how she must shut her eyes and go to sleep and dream of mountains and valleys and stars falling and parrots and antelopes and gardens, and everything lovely, she said . . . and saw that Cam was asleep. (p. 106)

Coupled clauses going nowhere, circling through the conjunction *and*, deck the swaddled skull in prettifying fancies to mesmerize the child into forgetfulness, rocking her on a see-saw of eternal rhythm. Consolatory though the story is, there is yet something in the narrative tone which mocks the rigmarole of fairies and bells, goats and antelopes; mocks it angrily as a downright lie. Indeed, there is an edge so keen in the narrative's pure mimicry of the sweet deceits of nursery lore as to suggest self-irony on the part of the author, for surely it is precisely Virginia Woolf's own narrative practice to phrase the ugly and threatening in a mellifluous language couched in hypnotic rhythms of incantation: *and everything lovely*, as Mrs Ramsay's anodyne voice decrees. We all know quite well, and Cam knows, that the skull is still there to be unpacked by Time, behind the curtain of imagery. It is as if Virginia Woolf's rending of the veil in Part Two of *To the Lighthouse* was her attempt to tear off that surface layer of artistic beauty through which she – like Shakespeare in his last plays – could bear to contemplate the most terrible facts of life and death, through a transformative lyricism which makes coral out of the bones of a dead father and plants pearls where his eyes have been. Nevertheless, Virginia Woolf has not succeeded in shedding the cloak: the habit of beauty dies hard, and the prose of 'Time Passes', however terrible the events it chronicles, remains an immaculate and limpid flow of English.

In the third Section of *To the Lighthouse*, the past is tested against the present and the present against the past, through reflection upon the faculty of memory and the semi-conscious assimilation of individuals' experience. In this postdeluvian phase, the green cloak has become the mother-element of the sea, the *mater maris* upon which the family completes its quest. Cam's hand is down in the streaming folds of the 'green swirls', her mind is transformed in the 'green light' and she reflects upon herself 'half transparent enveloped in a green cloak' (p. 169; and see p. 8). This passage, which is not present in the draft manuscript version which starts with James, is the product of Virginia Woolf's revision in the light of the whole text. We see her moving and adjusting symbols like counters on a board, for symmetry and development. Cam, who in the first Part, was a strange rushing little whirlwind of a girl 'off like a bird, bullet, or arrow' (p. 53) around her own private world, is in the third Part still a dreaming, inward being, dipping into the reservoir of the unconscious world as her hand takes the feel of the water. She is implicitly (though with significant differences) her mother's daughter. Modulations of the original symbolism surround her, insisting on her unconscious communion with all that was signified by the green cloak and has now been transferred to the green sea:

From her hand, ice cold, held deep in the sea, there spurted up a fountain of joy at the change, at the escape, at the adventure (that she should be alive, that she should be there). And the drops falling from this sudden and unthinking fountain of joy fell here and there on the dark, the slumbrous shapes in her mind . . . (p. 174)

The *fountain of joy* vaporously looks back (as the reader knows, though Cam cannot) to *this fountain and spray of life*, the life-force of her mother, which again looks back to *A fountain of gardens, a well of living waters* of the *Song of Solomon* (4:15 and see p. 25), the mystical identity of the beloved with the sources of all creation, to which the reader senses she has made return. Bringing the novel to its conclusion in September 1926, Virginia Woolf was aware of a difficulty of writing 'this last lap, in the boat . . . because the material is not so rich as it is with Lily on the lawn. I am forced to be more direct & more intense. I am making some use of symbolism, I observe. . .' (*Diary*, III, pp. 109–10).

The completion of the novel involved the retelling, by echo, rhythm and characters' vague recall of vestiges of their earlier symbolic stories: so that we perceive the vestigial traces of an older life in a younger, like beams of unknown light in an interior darkness. Cam, looking drowsily back at the island, feels that:

all those paths and terraces and bedrooms were fading and disappearing, and nothing was left but a pale blue censer swinging rhythmically this way and that across her mind. It was a hanging garden; it was a valley, full of birds, and flowers, and antelopes . . . She was falling asleep. (p. 188)

This is the inheritance of the cloak; but if that is so, the island (again, as the reader knows, though Cam cannot) is implicated as the death's head. Immunized by her acquisition of the tale-teller's art ('So we took a little boat, she thought . . .' [p. 174]), Cam has been hypnotized into a state of innocence in relation to too much reality and believes the illusion caused by distance to her eye-line ('They don't feel a thing there, Cam thought . . .' [p. 169]). We, having the benefit of a double vision hidden from Cam, see in close-up on the island not the nursery conjurations of birds and flowers and antelopes, but Mrs Ramsay's other bequest, Lily's state of unholy pain. By splitting herself between these two personae, the one representing her teenage self, the other in middle age (Lily is forty-four in Part Three, the author's exact age at the time of writing) Virginia Woolf can offer a complex sequence of measurements based on the ironic alternation of perspectives between the two figures – the one addicted to the refuge of tale-telling as escape to a vision wonderfully soporific, the other open-eyed in a postlapsarian world. Her art has to include the knowledge passed out to us in Part Two: the revelations of the mirror's-eye-view.

Section 6 of 'Time Passes' – the centre of the centre – concerns the deaths in the younger generation and the experience of the War. It is here that the author internalizes the mirror and ritually smashes it. The questors at the shore-line – artists and philosophers, we presume – are allured out by a false spring, seeking corroboration of their hopes for unity and accord with Nature, desiring a composing landscape:

to assemble outwardly the scattered parts of the vision within. In those mirrors, the minds of men, in those pools of uneasy water, in which clouds for ever turn and shadows form, dreams persisted . . . (p. 123)

93

The Platonistic mirror within searches to reflect an integrity in the cosmos which is lacking in man himself; the aim is a peaceful reconciliation of the seeing subject and the perceived object. Instead, omens and portents meet the imaginary questors' eyes – the apparition of an ashen ship out to sea, and 'a purplish stain upon the bland surface of the sea as if something had boiled and bled, invisibly, beneath' (p. 124). Here the apocalyptic implications of the text reach their height, evoking the trump of doom in the Book of Revelation:

8 And the second angel sounded, and as it were a great mountain burning with fire was cast into the sea: and the third part of the sea became blood;
9 And the third part of the creatures which were in the sea, and had life, died; and the third part of the ships were destroyed. (*Revelation* 8 : 8–9)

The star Wormwood is flung into the rivers and corrupts the fresh water in the 'fountains of waters' (8:10–11). In 'Time Passes' the blood-stained sea signals the moral filth of mankind and the War he has generated, mirrored in a bestial Nature such as Tennyson dreamt: 'Nature, red in tooth and claw' (*In Memoriam*, LVI), deriding man's pastoral and piscatory fancies of sympathies between the human and the natural (see pp. 101 ff.). When the mirror of contemplation smashes at the end of the section, so does the pathetic fallacy and all pastoral wishfulness, together with the reflections of art upon a pain-killing beauty, for 'to pace the beach was impossible; contemplation was unendurable; the mirror was broken' (p. 125). The echo of Tennyson's *Lady of Shalott* is unmistakable, as are countless remembrances of the laureate of doubt within the Platonizing mirror – and pool-imagery of these central sections: sorrow as a changeless reality that:

> knows no more of transient form
> In her deep self, than some dead lake
>
> That holds the shadow of a lark
> Hung in the shadow of a heaven
> (*In Memoriam* XVI)

To make this comparison is a useful reminder of the rootedness of Modernism in the psychomachia of a generation it denounced the believed itself to have outlived. *To the Lighthouse* is Virginia Woolf's latterday *In Memoriam*. Its sea is the same that Arnold heard at Dover, with the 'melancholy, long, withdrawing roar' (*Dover Beach*, line 25) and saw in *To Marguerite – Continued*: 'The unplumb'd, salt, estranging sea' (line 24). Its mirroring pool of reflection lies open, like the bereaved self in Tennyson's *In Memoriam*, to receive the full, faith-compelling dazzle of divine revelation, but is a 'dead lake' whose polluted waters contain no life of their own, but whose stagnancy makes for a perfect 'surface glassiness' (*To the Lighthouse*, p. 125) to reflect unreal images in its own unreality – the shadow of a lark in the shadow of a heaven. The sense of living at the end of the world, at a time of terrible, blood-stained chaos, surrounded by portents of destruction – epitomized by Yeats in his *Second Coming* – was not initiated but inherited and intensified by the War generation.

In the first draft, the Tennysonian mingling of apocalyptic and Platonist elements is even more evident than in the final version. The sixth Section of 'Time Passes' was originally Section 4, with the parentheses for the announcement of the family deaths a later addition. Originally, the author had a 'snout' thrust up from under the surface of the sea, associated with 'sharks' (*Holograph Manuscript*, p. 221): 'The black snout interfered with the whole composition' (p. 222). She denominates the mirrored images by the explicitly Platonist 'Semblances' and concludes 'and the snout broke the mirror' (sic). Although one can only be relieved that she deleted the embarrassingly incongruous animal nose from the final draft, the manuscript version permits us an X-ray of the primitive conception of the final composition. The bestial monster beneath the sea suggests (in the context of the massively apocalyptic symbolism and prophetic manner of the central Part) the beast that rose out of the sea in the Book of Revelation 'and upon his heads the name of blasphemy' (13:7). Within 'Time Passes' itself, it picks up a pattern of imagery which assimilates insentient and impersonal nature to an experience of inhuman (and sexually menacing) bestiality: the penetrating 'airs' which 'mount . . . nose . . . fumble . . . rub' their way into and round the house they will destroy (p. 118); the leviathan waves which are seen to mount one another and tumble into one another, to the confusion of all form, 'as if the universe were battling and tumbling, in brute confusion and wanton lust aimlessly by itself' (p. 125). This furore of contending elements is the Platonic *prima materia*, Milton's Chaos, the formless flux of unsettled matter which is both nature's womb and grave, with the addition of intimations of obscene and onanistic sexuality – a sexuality indistinguishable from warfare and violence. This horror of sexuality pervades Part Two of *To the Lighthouse* with hallucinatory force, and seems to spell out the implications of that sleeping or waking dream recorded by Virginia Woolf in *A Sketch of the Past* in which she saw 'a horrible face – the face of an animal, looking over her own shoulder into the mirror (see p. 77). The sea-vision of the central Part, with its revelation of a monstrous and inimical predatoriness under the surface of the planet we call home, is seen to corrupt all vision and all language. When Lily and Mr Carmichael return, with peacetime, to the Hebridean island, the house has been restored and cleansed of impurity. Lily, laying her head on the pillow for her first night's sleep in this new heaven and new earth hears murmuring 'Through the open window the voice of the beauty of the world' (p. 132). 'Gently' the waves break and enter her consciousness through the veil of sleep: 'tenderly' the light falls, suffusing itself through her closed lids. The passage reads like a cynical parody of the account of Virginia Woolf's primal memory, in which the child lies half asleep hearing the waves sough 'one, two, one, two' in her nursery at St Ives, and the little acorn on the blind makes its tiny sound in harmony with the sea's rhythm, respiring with the breeze (see p. 10). We have seen this primal memory transcribed into *To the Lighthouse* as a base of pre-conscious blessedness upon which the novel's emotion rests: a kind of wise nostalgia which teaches the art of making peace with the universe (see pp. 10 ff. above). But 'Time Passes' vitiates the memory; it corrupts the 'gentle' waves and the light that speaks so 'tenderly' to the lulled and unsuspicious eye, so that the very words make us wince in the final section of Lily's reverie. The voice of beauty has been exposed as a lie, complicit with the whole network of sense impressions in which the human creature is betrayed, like a child who is satisfied if a cloak be placed over a skull.

After such knowledge, what forgiveness? The novel is conceived as an 'elegy', and – using the ritual structure of pastoral elegy, a form in which, through symbolic and mythic modulations, hope is traditionally drawn by a simulation of organic processes from extreme pain, like a plant rooted in a grave – redemptive figures and symbols begin to flourish within the symbolism of Part Two itself, which should logically exclude them. But there are other, more down-to-earth answers. Since we started with tables, we might end with boots. Resurgent comedy in Part Three readjusts the perspectives. The wildly accelerating clock-hands of 'Time Passes' accommodate to the sobriety of daylight time, and on the word 'Awake', the last of Part Two (p. 133), the ghosts and phantasmal terrors go underground. Anxieties generated by 'tables' in the metaphysical realm (subject, object and the nature of reality) are dissipated on 'the blessed island of good boots' (p. 144). In the disintegrated family world After Mrs Ramsay, dominated by that unruly tantrum-thrower, the *paterfamilias*, there are voices, bangings, resentments and unease, and uncertainty about objects summarized in Nancy's 'What does one send to the Lighthouse?' (p. 137), provocative of all sorts of doubts. But the unsatisfactoriness of the household is common-or-garden; the turmoil and strife recognizably the familiar brew of the nuclear family unit with adolescents. In the delicious, poignant second Section, the full focus of tragi-comic vision is played on to the bereaved father sympathy-cadging from the reluctant Lily, a very poor substitute for the fountain of life itself from whom Mr Ramsay had become used to greedily drinking. There is a scrupulous and judicious fairness in Virginia Woolf's prose-style in relation to his flaws and glories; ironic moderation as she details and thus controls immoderate emotions. The father is recreated on a global scale as a monster of groans, which burst from him 'with the force of some primeval gust' (p. 142), a near cosmic ebullition to which 'any other woman *in the whole world*' (my emphasis) would have responded. This mock-heroic inflation is recorded laconically, together with the coded meanings of a whole repertoire and alphabet of sighs, expressive of a variety of claims: 'He sighed profoundly. He sighed significantly'. Lily's split response is signalled in the nausea at his 'sickly look' which keeps company in the same sentence with her attraction to 'his beautiful hands'. Mr Ramsay arrays himself in gestures and 'draperies of grief' like a Victorian funerary monument; the prose exposes his embarrassing ploys ruthlessly as he whines and totters, with every moment more infantile and less deserving of veneration, to the degree that, when his demand for sympathy is said to have 'poured and spread itself in pools at her feet' (p. 143), it is hard for a reader to refrain from inward animadversion to the phenomenon of infant bed-wetting and its attention-seeking function. Lily's refusal of the maternal obligation to clear up his unsightly mess, together with the guilt-feelings he has aroused and is playing on, are all too understandable.

But with one of those exquisite turns which characterize the narrative method of Part One, the mood suddenly reverses itself with Lily's sighting of Mr Ramsay's boots: '"What beautiful boots!" she exclaimed. She was ashamed of herself. To praise his boots when he asked her to solace his soul . . .' (p. 144). A cardinal rule for the reader of *To the Lighthouse* has been to appreciate that we are not to look for an engagement with objective reality but for subjective perceptions, a flow of consciousness which cerebrates all the raw material of perception into a version of itself. Under this rule, objects lose solidity, flesh its

97

mass and density, the stone is a thought-stone only and is not available to be kicked, for all exists in solution with the knower. Mr Ramsay's boots defy this rule. Like an island of substantiality in the ocean of thought and feeling, the boots achieve – as Lily admires them and Mr Ramsay expatiates upon their beauty, good sense and rarity-value, lifting his feet one at a time for inspection and then kneeling to teach the art of knot-tying – a wonderful reality for the reader. That reality can be tested by the degree to which the passage in question compels the reader to laugh out loud. The empty husks of gloves and shoes, cap, skirts, coats in wardrobes of Part Two (p. 120) are filled: an access of pure commonsense and ordinariness comes over the text of Part Three and grounds it in a sense of comic plenitude – the human foot reoccupying its boot and fitting to a nicety. As Lily and Mr Ramsay commune on these saving matters, Lily's sympathies are naturally liberated, and the loving homage she could not extend when he extorted it flows from her in silent benediction (too late, of course, as the fiction insists, arresting any tendency toward a thoroughly satisfactory conclusion of great or small affairs, by another cunningly ironic *volte face*). Objects, occasionally, can in a moment of vitality, leap out into an affirmation of their own reality, engendering a solution to the great issues in the simplest of encounters. As 'those wonderful boots' (p. 145) carry Mr Ramsay away on his quest, carrying the brown paper parcels (another token of substantiality weighing with pleasant heaviness upon the gauzy continuum of the novel's process of consciousness) Lily is naturally led round and back to the question of the table, which she remembers conjuring up ten years previously:

But what a face ... What had made it like that? Thinking, night after night, she supposed – about the reality of kitchen tables, she added, remembering the symbol which in her vagueness as to what Mr Ramsay did think about Andrew had given her. (He had been killed by the splinter of a shell instantly, she bethought her.) The kitchen table was something visionary, austere; something bare, hard, not ornamental. There was no colour to it; it was all edges and angles; it was uncompromisingly plain. But Mr Ramsay kept always his eyes fixed upon it, never allowed himself to be distracted or deluded ... He must have had his doubts about that table, she supposed; whether the table was a real table; whether it was worth the time he gave to it; whether he was able after all to find it. (pp. 145–6)

From the indubitable boots, with their practical quality of being there, and serviceable, and marking Mr Ramsay's entitlement to respect and his lovability, to the very dubious, spartan table which advertises itself by its relentless capacity for absence, is a step of compassion and understanding. As Lily gives him her silent tribute, Mr Ramsay leading his 'little company bound together' (p. 146) is processing beyond her horizon. There is a faintly Attic quality about this passage of recessional, like the scene on Keats's Grecian Urn, with its depopulation of a village in the far past toward some unknown ceremonial:

So they passed the edge of the lawn, and it seemed to Lily that she watched a procession go, drawn on by some stress of common feeling which made it, faltering and flagging as it was, a little company bound together and strangely impressive to her. (p. 145)

> Who are these coming to the sacrifice? . . .

> And, little town, thy streets for evermore
> Will silent be; and not a soul to tell
> Why thou are desolate, can e'er return.

(Keats *Ode on a Grecian Urn*, lines 31, 38–40)

Standing with Lily on the uncanny margin between present and past, the shadowy author of *To the Lighthouse* memorializes the closing phase of her own youth, saluting the shade of the father on his last voyage out.

4. Elegy

> Thou'lt come no more,
> Never, never, never, never, never!
> (*King Lear*, V. iii. 309–10)

There were boots and shoes; and a brush and comb left on the dressing-table, for all the world as if she expected to come back to-morrow. (She had died very sudden at the end, they said.) And once they had been coming, but had put off coming, what with the war, and travel being so difficult these days; they had never come all these years; just sent her money; but never wrote, never came . . . (*To the Lighthouse*, pp. 126–7)

Come back . . . coming . . . coming . . . never came . . . never came: 'come' and 'never' tear against each other, irreconcilable and absurd partners, the one a passionate invitation, the other an enforced relinquishment. Lear's *never* ticks out the second hand on the clock of eternity, emptying the lake of hell by thimblefuls of time. The monotony of loss tolls through the hypnotic repetitions whereby *To the Lighthouse* mourns its dead, protractedly, deferring its own conclusion, fine-spinning its ghosts until it can complete its process of mourning by acknowledgement of the fact that the living beings will 'come no more,/ Never'. When she named the genre of her work 'elegy' rather than 'novel', in her Diary, Virginia Woolf's Modernistic rebellion against the conventions of realistic fiction took the form of an acquiescence in the far more rigorous conventions of a poetic form that is as old as human love itself:

(But while I try to write, I am making up 'To the Lighthouse' – the sea is to be heard all through it. I have an idea that I will invent a new name for my books to supplant 'novel'. A new — by Virginia Woolf. But what? Elegy?) (*Diary*, III, p. 34)

This eager parenthesis demonstrates the unity of generic form with symbolic location in her conception of *To the Lighthouse*: the elegy for her is sea-music. Piscatory – that sub-genre of pastoral elegy, in which the shepherds are fishermen, their flocks the shoaling fish, their spiritual field the volatile surface of the sea of purgation, birth and death, their saviour the music-loving dolphin and their Ideal the Christ who walked the water – is the chosen mode of *To the Lighthouse*, with its trout and

100

minnows so strangely immersed in the human subconscious (p. 99), Nancy's crab the leviathan of the shore-line world (p. 72), Mr Ramsay tumbling backwards and walloping off like the great sea lion at the zoo (pp. 34–5), Macalister's boat, the fisherman and his boy, and the dying mackerel with a square cut out of its side for bait, tossed back negligently still alive into the common pool of pain (p. 167). The sign of the fish, the ancient emblem for the primitive Christians of Christ sacrificed, also signs this novel as a token of the mystery of creaturely life and suffering. Christ's Passion is an event frequently invoked by direct allusion but as an image of desecrating agony rather than as an act of mediation between God and man. The pain of loss, therefore, is raw and unatoned. Consolation is not available from a Heavenly source; it must be evoked from the ritual of grief itself.

Pastoral elegy has its roots in the Greek poetry Virginia Woolf so revered, and it is right to think of her work of the 'twenties as part of that neoclassical revival which characterized Modernism: the mock-Homeric *Ulysses*, Pound's activation of classical myth, H D's Hellenistic lyrics. The redemptive and consolatory aspects of *To the Lighthouse* are provided by a pre-Christian mythologizing of mother-love in terms of assimilation of the person of Mrs Ramsay to the corn- and flower-goddesses of classical myth, in a landscape whose wintry blight is rendered more clement by being viewed in a cyclical, seasonal context. Structurally, the novel works according to pastoral elegy's traditional fulfilment of an entire cycle of grief, involving a questioning of the structure of mortal life in the light of bereavement. It names, describes and pays tribute to the beloved in Part One; questions humanity's relationship to God, nature, art and history in Part Two; and finally obeys the generic responsibility of elegy not only to record and lament but to offer healing words for the rupture in the pattern of meaning which is implied by mortal loss, with the ceremonial visits of mourners to the place of loss (all the characters of Part Three, especially Lily, Mr Carmichael and Mr Ramsay), the introduction of voices and figures bearing partial consolation at intervals in the cycle (Mrs McNab in Part Two, Lily's visions and Cam's dream-world in Part Three, as well as the successful landing at journey's end), the transformation of the lost person into the *genius loci* of the sacred site, with intimations of new and transcendent life in some other world:

> Where were you, Nymphs, where were you,
> where when Daphnis died?

101

In the valley of Peneius?
In Pindus' pretty glade?
(Theocritus, 'Thyrsis' Lament for Daphnis',
Idylls, 1, c. 300 BC, *Greek Pastoral
Poetry*, p. 47)

Ah, when the mallows perish in the orchard,
or the green parsley, or the thickly blossoming dill,
they grow again, and live another year;
but we who are so great and strong, we men
who are so wise, as soon as we are dead,
at once we sleep, in a hole beneath the earth,
a sleep so deep, so long, with no end,
no reawakening. And so it is for you:
in the earth you shall lie, shrouded in silence;
whilst, if it pleases the Nymphs, a frog
may sing forever.
(Moschus, *Lament for Bion*, c. 150 BC, *Op. cit.*, p. 190)

All Musick sleepes when Death doth leade the dance,
And shepherds wonted solace is extinct.
(Spenser, *Shepheardes Calender*, XI, 105–6; 1590)

Fear no more the heat o' the sun,
      Nor the furious winter's rages;
Thou thy worldly task hast done,
      Home art gone, and ta'en thy wages;
Golden lads and girls all must,
      As chimney-sweepers, come to dust.
(*Cymbeline*, IV. ii. 258–63; 1610)

Where were ye, Nymphs, when the remorseless deep
Closed o'er the head of your loved Lycidas? . . .

Ay me! whilst thee the shores and sounding seas
Wash far away, where'er thy bones are hurled,
Whether beyond the stormy Hebrides,
Where thou perhaps under the whelming tide
Visit'st the bottom of the monstrous world . . .
(Milton, *Lycidas*, 50–1, 154–8; 1637)

Alas! that all we loved of him should be,
But for our grief, as if it had not been,
And grief itself be mortal. Woe is me!
Whence are we, and why are we? of what scene
The actors or spectators? Great and mean

Meet massed in death . . .

(Shelley, *Adonais*, st. 21; 1821)

Did Nature supplement what man advanced? Did she complete what he began? With equal complacence she saw his misery, condoned his meanness and acquiesced in his torture. (Virginia Woolf, *To the Lighthouse*, p. 125)

Pastoral in its pure form has always confirmed and celebrated the amity between man and nature, its sympathy with his pain, endorsement of his aspirations and its seasonal calendar of life which fitly matches his own. But pastoral elegy by its very nature discountenances this blithe dream by recording a disjunction between man and nature: the herbs revive from the same root year by year, notes Moschus, but our die-back is final. Pastoral elegy points to the unnaturalness that vitiates nature and makes an enemy of the mother-world: short life, unfulfilled hopes, nature's indifference to man's complaints. It probes the wound: 'Where were you, Nymphs?' asks Theocritus in his native Greek; and this is remembered by Virgil in his 'Gallus' eclogue, 'Where were you, gentle Naiads?' (*Eclogues*, X. 9–10); and both are recalled by Milton casting around for the reason for Lycidas' drowning, 'Where were ye, Nymphs?' Elegists make a human chain across time, protesting, querying, seeking illumination in a universalizing voice, the act of commemoration being a corporate stand against Time itself. To take Virginia Woolf at her word and to set *To the Lighthouse* at the end of this tradition – to translate her, as it were, into Greek – is to elucidate within a two-thousand year old tradition both the formal principles and the spirit and mood of the novel, with its Attic rigour and the powerful, nostalgic sweetness of its song. If to be Modernist was to be self-proclaimingly revolutionary, then part of the revolutionary implication of Virginia Woolf's novels of the 1920s was to remind us that there is nothing new under the sun.

In particular, reading *To the Lighthouse*, readers may find themselves haunted by Milton's *Lycidas*, not only for its theme of death by water and the 'washing' of 'shores and sounding seas' throughout the poem (see p. 102) and the suggestion of a Hebridean location (line 156) but also for the irregular verse-forms of fluid stanzas whose turns and counter-turns resemble in their emotional flow the wave-like motion of unequal sections in *To the Lighthouse*. The questors' sighting of 'the silent apparition of an ashen-coloured ship' (p. 124) in 'Time Passes' suggests less Coleridge's *Ancient Mariner* than Milton's 'fatal and perfidious bark/ Built in the eclipse, and rigged with curses dark' (100–1): the ship of death as the curse on man, the hereditary taint of mortality his birthright. *Lycidas* too is a shore-line poem, looking back for its inspiration through Virgil to the composing voices of the Greeks: Theocritus, Bion, Moschus echo one another through his lines. But *Lycidas* as an artistic influence on a modern elegist who is a woman presents a problem rather than a solution. Milton's education was such as to equip him for his high calling. Virginia Woolf, denied the privileged, class-based formal education to which her brothers had automatic access, sat down and taught herself Greek, with a minimum of external help. If a reader of her essays is struck not only by her profound culture and breadth of reading but also by what can only be called an exceptional level of erudition, that is a testament of character and commitment in a more meaningful way than it could have been for her husband or brothers. Barred by her gender from the very lawns of Oxbridge, Virginia Woolf relates in *A Room of One's Own* (1929) that, as a lady, she was refused access to the College Library unless 'accompanied by a Fellow of the College or furnished with a letter of introduction' (p. 9). The work which she was intent on consulting was, she tells us, the manuscript of Milton's *Lycidas*, to check authorial revisions.

Lamb wrote how it shocked him to think it possible that any word in *Lycidas* could have been different from what it is. To think of Milton changing the words of that poem seemed to him a sort of sacrilege. This led me to remember what I could of *Lycidas* and to amuse myself with guessing which word it could have been that Milton had altered, and why. It then occurred to me that the very manuscript itself which Lamb had looked at was only a few hundred yards away . . . (*A Room of One's Own*, pp. 8–9)

However, blocking the Virginia Woolf persona's way stands a college official, 'like a guardian angel barring the way with a flutter of black gown instead of white wings' (p. 9), a clear ironic allusion to the Miltonic Paradise to which Eve's daughter is, in the nicest possible way, being shown the door. In the literary garden of the patriarchs, tradition keeps its sacred texts sequestered from lapsed female eyes. The female inheritor of the tradition is therefore disallowed her birthright, which she has to steal to make her own.

If this was so with the Miltonic elegy, it was far more true of the Greek and pre-Christian originals of the tradition. The English language is our mother tongue, which we receive (despite current feminist definitions of language as essentially a patriarchal construct, which I think misconceived) from the lips of our mothers so that it is doubly a female birthright. To appropriate Milton from the collegiate fathers can therefore be regarded as a liberation of what has been usurped. But the Greek language and literature which were for Virginia Woolf the essence of the modern literary inheritance, required a more daring raid on the male sequestrators to make them one's own, for the classics are dead languages and at the heart of public school male privilege. Virginia Woolf's notebooks, novels and essays reveal a deep and yearning allegiance to the Greek inheritance. In their literature lay clues and messages concerning the most occult enigmas of human life; their song was timeless and impersonal. We may see Virginia Woolf's most radical experiment in fiction, *The Waves*, as an attempt to emulate that spirit, in its impersonal play of choric voices. When she lay ill and hallucinating in periods of breakdown, the birds sang to her in the Greek language, as they did to Septimus in *Mrs Dalloway*:

they sang in voices prolonged and piercing in Greek words, from trees in the meadow of life beyond a river where the dead walk, how there is no death. (p. 28)

The message of the birds is at once terrible and consolatory, as in elegy; it issues from the Elysian fields across the Styx and relates the same message that the elegist must strive to voice: 'Weep no more, woeful shepherds, weep no more,/ For Lycidas your sorrow is not dead' (*Lycidas*, 165–6); 'Dido is dead, but into heaven hent' (*Shepheardes Calender*, XI. 169); 'Peace, peace! he is not dead' (*Adonais*, 39, line 343). The birds on the Elysian trees articulate unutterable pain like the raped, tongueless maiden of Greek mythology, Philomela, with a purifying sweetness, T. S. Eliot's 'So rudely forc'd./ Tereu' (*The Waste Land*, III. 205–6).

An essay in *The Common Reader* (1925) entitled 'On Not Knowing Greek' attributes primacy not to Greek literature but to the Greek language. Greek stood as a code for conceptions which modern living languages could not articulate. Its constraint, ambiguities, spareness and universality of utterance fascinated Virginia Woolf by seeming to harbour sphinx-like secrets about ourselves, our earth and how we stand to the gods. By being 'dead', its mystery was enhanced. It had attained a static, self-reflexive quality as if it stood as a memorial to itself. We could lay this linguistic nostalgia beside the backward-yearning gaze of *To the Lighthouse*: 'But the dead, thought Lily ... Oh the dead! she murmured ... They are at our mercy' (p. 162). Greek too, as Virginia Woolf understood, is at our mercy, open to our interpretation as no living language or person can be. Yet she trusted her intuition that the Greek language has 'meaning ... just on the far side of language. It is the meaning which in moments of astonishing excitement and stress we perceive in our minds without words' (*The Common Reader*, Vol. I, p. 7). *To the Lighthouse* tries to throw a net over this 'x' extrinsic to language, the indeterminate 'something', 'thing', 'life', 'it'. But what is extrinsic to living English Virginia Woolf identified as intrinsic to dead Greek – which, however, is by virtue of its death unknowable. We 'wish to know Greek, try to know Greek, feel for ever drawn to Greek, for ever mak[e] up some notion of the meaning of Greek' (p. 1). This passionate sentence records her hunger for that élite and occult language which was off the young lady's syllabus, forbidden fruit being all the more precious a possession when she had appropriated it to her own use because she had taken it for herself and made it her own by such strenuous efforts.

Paradoxically, Greek – the province of the custodial father-culture – represented a return to a way of knowing and seeing which preceded patriarchy and offered a radical (and potentially feminist) alternative to the male Trinity of Father, Son and Holy Ghost, a male priesthood and value systems. In leading her elegy toward the ritual therapy of consolation, the author of *To the Lighthouse* incorporates mythic elements to complete the cycle of grief, especially the fertility myth of Demeter and Persephone, the corn goddess and spring maiden, whose temple at Eleusis gave spiritual light and hope to generations of pilgrim-initiates in the Hellenic world. Allusion to the Greek mystery-religions, defensively ironic or implied with the lightest touch of glancing obliquity, infuses a cryptic hope into the process of *To the Lighthouse*, enclosing its round of desolation (the furore of seasons in Part Two) in the difficult, obscure but real hope of human growth: through the womanly creativity of the mother, Mrs Ramsay, and the virginal art of the spinster Lily – and not only this, but through the dignity, honour and chastity with which the thoughtful voices of the elegy, including the narrative voice, take up the burden of mourning, inquiry and remedial articulation. We emerge from reading the work in a mood not unlike that inspired by Greek tragedy: with the sense of having witnessed and participated in a corporate endeavour to clarify and be reconciled to the perplexities of the mortal condition. The blight on the land in Part Two is never atoned or forgiven, but, sacrificially, *it is finished*; Demeter's curse on the natural world is lifted in Part Three, and the process of human reflection can continue into a new generation. This remedial articulation is conducted primarily through the play of symbolic and mythic elements through the mourning voice of Lily as it strives toward a final composure. The threnody for Mrs Ramsay belongs to her, and it is through her reading of the new reality that the reader is brought to a tentative reconciliation with things as they are – the stabler serenity which must be reached before the elegist can put down the pen and complete the work, having done justice to the past sufficiently to concede that it *is* past: the emotion of forward-looking renewed interest in the created and creative world that concludes Milton's *Lycidas* – 'To-morrow to fresh woods, and pastures new' (193).

The reign of the corn-goddess had been restored to poetry in the generation of classicists preceding Virginia Woolf's: it is exemplified in the anti-Christian classicism of Swinburne in his *Hymn to Proserpina*, but also through the work of mythographic sociologists such as Frazer, whose *Golden Bough* so grasped the imagination of T. S. Eliot, and especially the researches of Jane Ellen Harrison, whose *Ancient Art and Ritual* Virginia Woolf records consulting in her Reading Notes for 1923–4 (*Virginia Woolf's Reading Notebooks*, ed. B. R. Silver, p. 103). She is at one with her friend E. M. Forster in revering Demeter above all other gods, and in mythologizing the persons of elderly maternal women in constellations of emblems traditionally attributed to Demeter: Mrs Wilcox in *Howard's End* carries insignia of hay from her meadow and flowers from her garden; Mrs Moore in *A Passage To India*, where the daughter-figure Miss Quested attests to 'rape' in the 'underworld' of a cave, is regenerated as 'Esmiss Esmoor', Hindu mother-goddess. These figures parallel Virginia Woolf's Mrs Ramsay, mature, emotive *matres dolorosae*, resplendent in a riddling way beyond the banality of their articulations, a source and terminus of hope and desire. In 'Cnidnus', published in *Abinger Harvest* (1936), Forster spoke of his feelings for Demeter:

Demeter, alone among gods, has true immortality. The others continue, perchance, their existence, but are forgotten, because the time came when they could not be loved. But to her, all over the world, rise prayers of idolatory from suffering men as well as suffering women, for she has transcended sex. And poets too, generation after generation, have sung in passionate incompetence of the hundred-flowered Narcissus and the rape of Persephone . . . (*Abinger Harvest*, p. 172)

For Forster, the corn-goddess has retained meaning because she presents an icon of lovability; she is real in proportion as she fills a human need, as a psychic content and as a hope for an ultimate benignity in a universe of suffering which she shares with humanity as fellow-victim, and seeks to comprehend as fellow-questor. The social anthropologists of the late nineteenth and early twentieth centuries who excavated the field of ancient myth, saw by the light of the new secular sciences and offered their findings as valuable in shedding a subtle illumination on the universal human psyche, its tribal and individual needs, and the possibility of healing for its neuroses and transformation in the light of ancient unconscious wisdoms. The Demeter story affirms the potential creativity of deep affliction; the spirit's renewal from old impairment; a feminine vision of deity and the supremacy of female creativity as the supreme good on the planet; a sense of benignity in the universe and in the soul which, though not omnipotent like the Father-God (in whose responsibility for evil it does not share) is accessible, clement, enduring, nurturing. The myth gave to Virginia Woolf as a woman elegist access to imagery of spiritual transformation which does not pretend, as Christianity does, to reconcile Divine Omnipotence with Divine Love. The inadequacy of the Scriptural solution to the problem of pain addressed by *To the Lighthouse* is insisted on by Mrs Ramsay as she communes with herself in Part One. Disgusted with herself for mouthing the platitude, 'We are in the hands of the Lord' (p. 62), she goes on to insist, 'How could any Lord have made this world?', meaning any Lord worthy to be worshipped, for her meditation implies that an evil Lord might well be suspected of the unjust Creation. It is Mrs Ramsay's quest from the first Section to alleviate the suffering of the poor and the sick (the victims of that Creation). Charles Tansley waits in the 'poky little house' of the sick woman whom Mrs Ramsay is visiting and hears her voice above saying 'they must keep the windows open and the doors shut, ask at the house for anything they wanted' (p. 18). Toward the end of the book, Lily recalls seeing Mrs Ramsay return from such visits, when she had been moved to think that 'eyes that are closing in pain have looked on you. You have been with them there' (p. 181). This gracious balance of phrasing closes a paragraph with the awe of an epitaph: it reverences a more than human concern for fellow suffering and apostrophizes 'you /You' as a mediatorial figure outside the normal compass. Like Demeter, Mrs Ramsay is enlisted on the side of marriage, fertility and procreation. The mother of an innumerable brood, 'she would have liked always to have had a baby' (p. 57), though she is aware that the ruthless maternal instinct condemns each new child to pain and death in a universe where 'There was always a woman dying of cancer' (p. 58). Her terrible refrain that 'people must marry; people must have children' (p. 58); 'Did that not mean that they would marry? . . . They must marry!' (p. 68); 'William must marry Lily' (p. 97) takes on a relentless quality in context, its imperious force going beyond the domineering myopia of a narrow-minded Victorian matron, to suggest an unappeasable quality as of a law-giving goddess. The floral motif is almost always nearby when this chorus is voiced. When she concludes that 'William must marry Lily', it is for the weakly absurd reason (reading in realistic terms) that 'Lily is so fond of flowers' (p. 97). But Lily, true to the emblematic suggestions of her name, is no candidate for the flower-maiden. The deflowered springtime maiden raped away to the underworld is her own daughter Prue, 'given in marriage that May' and dying in pregnancy that summer. The role of the grieving mother, who has pre-deceased her daughter, seems to pass into the fertile natural world itself, mourning her daughter, as Prue in her springtime exposure to the mortality which will enter her in the very seeds of the sexual act has been assimilated to virgin nature awaiting its future:

The spring without a leaf to toss, bare and bright like a virgin fierce in her chastity, scornful in her purity, was laid out on fields wide-eyed and watchful and entirely careless of what was done or thought by the beholders. (pp. 122–3)

Moreover, softened and acquiescent, the spring with her bees humming and gnats dancing threw her cloak about her, veiled her eyes, averted her head, and among passing shadows and flights of small rain seemed to have taken upon her a knowledge of the sorrows of mankind. (p. 123)

One way of 'seeing' in our mind's eye something of the artistic method by which Virginia Woolf incorporates mythic material by moving her perspective from the mythologized individual to the personified natural world and its seasons might be to imagine a filmed interpretation of the novel in which the camera would pan between the white fear and virgin pride of Prue before her marriage 'bare and bright like a virgin fierce in her chastity' and the frosted natural scene at the turning of the year; the cloaked softness of Prue in her pregnancy and the same ripeness and openness to mortal pain in the natural scene. In entering the earth through death, Prue becomes indistinguishably one with her mother. Lily, who has centred all her questioning in Part One on the person of Mrs Ramsay, must address, implore and interrogate earth, air and water in Part Three, locating the person as 'spirit of place' in the time-honoured manner of elegy. The task of the elegist is to convert the

sense of the universe as a place of interment from a locus of fear and
threat to one of containment and safe-keeping, Shelley's 'He is made
one with Nature: there is heard/ His voice in all her music' (*Adonais*,
42, lines 370–1). This turning-point inaugurates the final Consolation
and permits the transference of the poet's mantle from the dead friend
to his successor: or, in the case of *To the Lighthouse* from the lost
creatrix to her 'daughter', Lily, who as artist-creator can put the
finishing touch to her picture.

Such a transformation of personal to mythic elements is initiated in
the novel, however, long before the second Section begins to assimilate
the person of the dead Mrs Ramsay by delicate manipulations of symbol
and allusion. Part One is essential in preparing the reader to accept
such a modulation as artistically logical. Its function is to persuade the
reader that there is more to Mrs Ramsay than is literally expressible by
the significations on the page; to create her for us as a mystery with
strange and rather frightening powers at the same time as it insists on
her acceptability on the social level as an ordinary woman with her own
particular vanities and vagaries. The medium of creative illusion is, of
course, narrative voice or voices which urge upon us allegations which
carry all the more conviction for the absence of an omniscient authoriz-
ing voice to validate or contradict them. *To the Lighthouse* is, at the
moments of greatest revelation, the most profoundly evasive and reticent text. Because it never embroils itself in matters of fact, its apologetic
system of one-sided guesswork and impressionism can put almost
anything over on its reader. 'The poet,' said Sidney, 'never affirmeth'
(*Defence of Poetry*, p. 102). But, more crucially for this novel, she denies
nothing either, and some of the eye-beams she allows to play upon the
page have such a startling power and intensity that we are beguiled into
believing that this is the right light to judge by. The climax of Part
One, the memorable set piece of Mrs Ramsay's dinner-party, is a
perfect instance of this conjuring-trick technique brought about by
authorial escapology. Lily's-eye-view comes to carry overwhelming
conviction as the episode develops:

There was something frightening about her. She was irresistible. Always she got
her own way in the end, Lily thought. Now she had brought this off – Paul and
Minta, one might suppose, were engaged. Mr Bankes was dining here. She put a
spell on them all, by wishing, so simply, so directly; and Lily contrasted that
abundance with her own poverty of spirit, and supposed that it was partly that
belief (for her face was all lit up – without looking young, she looked radiant) in
this strange, this terrifying thing, which made Paul Rayley, the centre of it, all of

a tremor, yet abstract, absorbed, silent. Mrs Ramsay, Lily felt, as she talked about the skins of vegetables, exalted that, worshipped that; held her hands over it to warm them, to protect it, and yet, having brought it all about, somehow laughed, led her victims, Lily felt, to the altar. (p. 94)

We read here a partial reading, as the text self-deprecatingly three times goes out of its way to confess with the modifying phrases, 'Lily thought ... Lily felt ... Lily felt'. Nobody but Lily felt like this. Mr Bankes is relishing his succulent *Boeuf en Daube*. Paul is on fire with thoughts of Minta, and Eros. Mr Ramsay is laughing with Minta. Charles Tansley is eating, presumably, and the text registers none of his perceptions at this moment. But it is hard, almost impossible, for a reader to resist the pressure of what 'Lily thought ... Lily felt'. The short, generalizing sentences have a piercing conclusiveness, entering us with Lily's sharp emotion. They mediate a quality of terror in relation to Mrs Ramsay – 'frightening ... irresistible' – which the novel has already gone far to endorse, not least in the cluster of mock-Homeric similes which precede this passage and which obviously represent the novel's voice rather than that of any specific individual. 'And, like some queen ... she went down' (pp. 77–8); 'as a sailor not without weariness ...' (p. 79); 'So, when there is a strife of tongues ...' (p. 84). Likening small things to great is conventionally supposed to inflate the small until it bursts with its own pretension; mock-heroic pleases by its grotesque deformation of traditional perspectives as to what is great and petty, with a view to reasserting them. Virginia Woolf's mock-Homeric similes, however, are as dextrously and cunningly insidious as anything she wrote. Their irony is defensive and exploitative, taking the reader off guard while it insinuates a female revision of the Homeric glorification of machismo – war and feasts, perilous sailings-forth and monster-hunts. Mrs Ramsay is established as the queen descending, the dying sailor on his homeward odyssey, the peace-maker at the council table, in a renovated epic ethos which extols the arts of peace, and the labours of womankind – giving meals, knitting clothing, receiving guests and caring for their needs – Penelope's sanctum preferred over Odysseus's wayfaring, as the truer human odyssey. It is neo-Homeric rather than mock-Homeric. 'She put a spell on them all,' thinks Lily in the quoted passage, and this phrasing, which puts a magical and Circean gloss on the power we have witnessed in action, which seems only to have to wish and the thing is done, is also with some craft endorsed by the surrounding text – in, for instance, the action of the 'antennae' which we view as supernaturally

111

entering into the sealed minds of the guests, 'like a light stealing under water . . .' (p. 99). Another layer of suggestiveness emerges in the visual image Lily throws forward to the reader – the face 'all lit up . . . radiant', the hands held over the shrine of Eros to exalt a sacrifice. The image develops into a bodying-forth of priestly power, the lurid lighting giving a numinous aura to the high priestess, who seems to act on behalf of a cruel deity – *Venus genetrix*, perhaps, demanding human sacrifice. This presentation of the dinner-party as corresponding to an ancient pagan festival is again endorsed by the predominant image patterns of the Section: Mrs Ramsay's fantasy of the dish of fruit in the candle-light as Neptune's banquet, Bacchus's fruit at the orgy, under torchlight (p. 90); her sense of 'celebrating a festival' of Eros, in which the lovers 'entering into illusion glittering eyed, must be danced round with mockery, decorated with garlands' (p. 93). Cumulative suggestion stealthily builds into the reader's consciousness a double sense of the party. On the one hand it is a commonplace occasion in which conversation of a deplorable level of banality takes place and the hostess is applying her social arts in a horribly evident manner at one end of the table. On the other, it is a candle-lit shadow of all the acts of communion round a table, all the festivals of sacrificial eating-together that have ever taken place since society began. The inner voices of Mrs Ramsay and Lily concur in viewing the occasion in such a light, and the symbolic matrix in which their perceptions are set help to privilege Lily's voice as it dwells on the mysterious and terrible element in Mrs Ramsay which, with her death, will be assimilated into the mythic structure more fully. It is worth reminding ourselves, too, that the festival involves a real sacrifice: Part Three discloses scathingly (through the eyes of the votaress of the virgin life, Lily) that the marriage engineered and celebrated by Mrs Ramsay so ruthlessly turns out to be an abject failure.

One well-attested phase of the cycle of mourning is the necessary effort that must be made by the bereaved person to distance herself from the one whose loss she mourns, recognizing his faults, fighting the idealization which is also a natural response to loss. The griever undergoes periods of anger and hostility to the lost person: she criticizes and belittles him to focus him smaller than that telephoto lens of bereavement allows which fills the entire horizon with the beloved face. She casts judgement, blaming him for many things, not least his departure which is thought of as a willed truancy. Recovery depends on such exorcism to cut the cord of dependency. Utterance is often found to be a part of healing: putting forth the experience in language gives it away and helps to free the sufferer. The genre of pastoral elegy has always known these facts of the psyche and ritualized many of them as part of its structure. As the mode was passed down through the Romantics to Virginia Woolf's predecessors, its therapeutic potency for the individual mourner became centralized as an important part of the convention: Tennyson's 'use in measured language' performs a 'sad mechanic exercise,/ Like dull narcotics, numbing pain' (*In Memoriam*, V), but at the end of the poem the work of words has had a more than ephemerally analgesic effect. It has pushed out the beloved from his tyrannical dominance of the inner world. Articulation has 'mingle(d) all the world with thee' (*In Memoriam*, CXXIX):

> Thy voice is on the rolling air;
>   I hear thee where the waters run;
>   Thou standest in the rising sun,
> And in the setting thou art fair.
>
> (CXXX)

Banished as *genius loci* of the pastoral scene according to the time-honoured pattern of elegy, the beloved releases the lover to a less hurtful, more quietly cherishing love. Virginia Woolf bore witness that the writing of *To the Lighthouse* fulfilled this therapeutic function of elegy: it allowed the trespassing ghost of her mother a painless exit from the daughter's usurped spirit by offering her a place of safe-keeping between the covers of a book:

Until I was in the forties – I could settle the date by seeing when I wrote *To the Lighthouse*, but am too casual here to bother to do it – the presence of my mother obsessed me. I could hear her voice, see her, imagine what she would do or say as I went about my day's doings. She was one of the invisible presences who after all play so important a part in every life. (*A Sketch of the Past, Moments of Being*, p. 93)

I used to think of him & mother daily; but writing The Lighthouse, laid them in my mind. And now he comes back sometimes, but differently. (I believe this to be true – that I was obsessed by them both, unhealthily; & writing of them was a necessary act.) (*Diary*, III, p. 208)

However, this 'necessary act' differs from the necessariness attributed to the composition of elegy by poets in the formal tradition of pastoral elegy. That tradition asserts a formalized tribute on behalf of a community, rather in the way that the solemn rites of the funeral service commemorate the life and acknowledge the death of a fellow being considered as a human soul rather than an individualized being. Pastoral elegy commends and formally renounces an idealized or generalized image in a voice which aspires to universality by its assimilation of the voices of its entire generic past. The writing of *Lycidas* is a 'necessary act' to Milton because 'He must not float upon his wat'ry bier/ Unwept, and welter to the parching wind,/ Without the meed of some melodious tear' (12–14). There is a sacred poetic duty of commemoration, on behalf of all writers and readers of poetry. Virginia Woolf was subject to no such obligation. *To the Lighthouse*, answering a need inner and subjective, takes advantage of the generic commitment of the novel to individualism and the subjective speaking voice – its roots in Protestant reverence for self-confessing singularity – and its conventions of realistic fidelity, to counter its idealizations with representation of the quirks and oddities, failings and inadequacies of those it mourns. We have spoken of Virginia Woolf, as she did herself, as an author whose Modernistic spirit emancipated her from the obsequiousness of the realistic novel to character, plot and verisimilitude; but until *The Waves*, that revolutionary dead-end in which the novel was de-personalized into a choric phantom of itself, a high degree of veri-similitude in fact remains in her fictions, earthing and defining the more abstract material. The extent to which *To the Lighthouse* realized a recognizable image of the author's dead mother and father to the point of an embarrassing likeness is reflected in Virginia Woolf's frequent anxieties during composition to think 'how all these people will read it & recognize poor Leslie Stephen & beautiful Mrs Stephen in it' (*Diary*, III, p. 61), a prognostication which made her feel 'rather queer' and was confirmed by her sister's haunted reaction:

Anyhow it seemed to me that in the first part of the book you have given a portrait of mother which is more like her to me than anything I would ever have conceived possible. It is almost painful to have her so raised from the dead . . . You have given father too I think as clearly, but perhaps, I may be wrong, that isn't quite so difficult . . . it is so shattering to find oneself face to face with these two again that I can hardly consider anything else. (Spalding, *Vanessa Bell*, p. 219)

This fictional licence to realize the minutiae of character on the page lent a power of catharsis to the novelist adaptor of elegy lacked by her poetic predecessors. She can focus a complex image of Mrs Ramsay in which glory coexists with banality; maternal bounty and integrity share space with mean thoughts, vanities and class-bound social manipulativeness. The prose at once idealizes and undercuts its own idealizations, detaching the image of the too-beloved mother and terribly lovable father from the creative self, with every stroke of the pen. The pen cuts away the tissue which had 'unhealthily' fused to root her to the posthumous effigies of the parents, by acts of criticism, feats of mockery, ironization and covert (in the case of the mother) condemnation. The art of this deflation has a subtle doubleness: it in fact functions to preserve, rather than to destroy the act of worship offered as the author's homage to the goddess-mother, by casting that image upon the reader's mind along with the other image, which can be criticized and cut down to size, judged to be of its time and consigned to the past. Lily performs on the part of the author this work of detachment and readjustment of perspective in Part Three in the paragraph of the elegy which is dominated by the refrain 'But the dead . . . Oh the dead' (p. 162). She acknowledges the unpalatable fact that 'one pitied them, one brushed them aside, one had even a little contempt for them'. In her mind, she mocks Mrs Ramsay's 'limited, old-fashioned ideas' and thinks with spiteful scorn of how she would like to tell Mrs Ramsay that everything has gone against her wishes, the Rayleys' bad marriage, her profession of singleness and art. 'They're happy like that; I'm happy like this. Life has changed completely.' Dancing on the grave in this self-affirming manner represents a partial liberation from the *Totentanz* of the central Sections of *To the Lighthouse*; but, as she goes on to realize, this exultant stance of independence from the antediluvian standards of the Victorian world-view is really a measure of the hold Mrs Ramsay has over her.

She had felt now she could stand up to Mrs Ramsay – a tribute to the astonishing power that Mrs Ramsay had over one Do this, she said, and one did it. Even her shadow at the window with James was full of authority. (p. 163)

In the third Part, the process of Lily's amendment, so that she is empowered to put the finishing touch to her *own* picture – a testament to how she is happy as she is in a life that has changed completely – is presented as an oscillation between the two images of Mrs Ramsay, the authority she must outgrow and the mortal goddess she must worship. The final Part is a long-drawn-out movement toward a point where justice can be done to the dead, a regretful process of moving into a position, or set of positions in relation to the image of the lost person, so that Lily can be content to say goodbye and turn away into her own future. On the boat, moving out to sea, Cam parallels this adaptation in her oscillation between divergent attitudes to her father, who more and more comes to impersonate for the reader the still, silent figure of a personage in a dream. The author draws him back into the strange realm of the past; he is viewed remotely through an eye of inquiry whose solicitations can as little as Lily's ('why was it so short, why was it so inexplicable ...' [p. 167]) be answered at this distance. The journey is made to appear, with its archetypal seas, becalmed and then racing, and its inscrutable protagonist who seems to go out to sea like a funerary god on a floating coffin, like a journey in Time rather than Space. Virginia Woolf can let go of her father by stages, returning his borrowed shadow to the past where it belongs. A multiple play of eye-beams, of wonderful mathematical subtlety, enables this process of letting-go to succeed. It is as if Virginia Woolf at the age of forty-five throws a sequence of projections of herself on to the page – Lily at forty-four, looking out to sea to Cam at eighteen, looking to the father in his seventies. Only by this time-travel along a relay of eye-lines can the necessary valedictory be fully and finally said. At the same time, and moving along the same axes, the author can make a progressive departure from Talland House and St Ives, the cocoon of childhood which maturity must forfeit.

But Cam could see nothing. She was thinking how all those paths and the lawn, thick and knotted with the lives they had lived there, were gone; were rubbed out; were past; were unreal, and now this was real ... (p. 155)

It was like that then, the island, thought Cam, once more drawing her fingers through the waves. She had never seen it from out at sea before. It lay like that on the sea, did it, with a dent in the middle and two sharp crags, and the sea swept in there, and spread away for miles and miles on either side of the island. It was very small; shaped something like a leaf stood on end. (p. 174)

She gazed back over the sea, at the island. But the leaf was losing its sharpness. It was very small; it was very distant. The sea was more important now than the shore. (p. 176)

This recessional parallels the recessive vision permitted to Lily of the mythologized figures of Mrs Ramsay and Prue into the Elysian fields. Mr Ramsay is assimilated to earth, looking in the closing stages 'very old', 'like some old stone lying on the sand' (p. 186) as he moves toward the 'rock' which is the final word of his journey (p. 191). There is the suggestion for the reader that his life, being nearly run through (the elegy allowing that it should be so) is turning or returning to the monumental basis of things – Emily Brontë's 'eternal rocks beneath'. Mrs Ramsay, together with Prue in a climactic sequence of allusions to the mother–daughter duality of the Demeter–Persephone myth, is assimilated to air – the vision of the light, quick figure 'raising to her forehead a wreath of white flowers with which she went':

It was strange how clearly she saw her, stepping with her usual quickness across fields among whose folds, purplish and soft, among whose flowers, hyacinths or lilies, she vanished. (p. 168)

This vision, with its ambiguous implications both bridal and funerary (see p. 12), was recast two days running in the manuscript draft. The first points out that antidotes grow by the sources of pain 'dock leaves ... beside nettles' (*Holograph Manuscript*, p. 303) in the natural world, and emphasizes the 'majesty with which taking her way among the dead she had raised and fitted to her forehead white flowers in a crown' (p. 303). Later she is explicitly named as 'the Bride of Death', assimilating the mother to the daughter Persephone, bride of Dis, the god of the underworld. In conception, as the later obliterated detail about the proximity of dock leaves to nettles in the natural world implies, the rich mythological material which characterizes the conclusion of the novel corresponds with the flower passages of pastoral elegy:

> Bid amaranthus all his beauty shed,
> And daffodillies fill their cups with tears,
> To strew the laureate hearse where Lycid lies.
> (*Lycidas*, 149–51)

Amaranthus, from the Greek root verb 'not-quenched-light-or-flame' is called to shed his red spired flowers into the grave, signifying an immortalizing but inconclusive hope. The flower passage in *Lycidas* for all its tender beauty is acknowledged by its poet as a failure: 'false surmise' (153), for corrupted nature cannot restore the beloved, though it may mourn and preserve his memory. Planted deep in Milton's elegy is also the hyacinth, 'that sanguine flower inscribed with woe' (106). The 'sanguine' flower which is also a *memento mori* in *To the Lighthouse* grew from the blood of Hyacinthus in the fertility myth; on its face the Greeks read the inscription 'AI', Apollo's lamentation at his accidental killing of his favourite with his quoit. Virginia Woolf plants this emblematic flower with the lily, to mark the passing of Mrs Ramsay and to signify her transformation to a veiled ulterior world of significations, where the burial ground is refocused as the root-bed of new life.

Lily, the source and witness of this visionary transformation, reflects herself into a modest role in the myth, for the hyacinth which keeps company with her namesake, the lily, image of vestal purity and the cool flower of death, was also understood by the Greeks to resemble the lily – a broken-stemmed lily that hangs its head. As in *Lycidas*, the passages of floral metamorphosis seem to offer only limited comfort, but their helpfulness is real. They provide a way of seeing departure (and repeating it at will so that the vanishing-point is never final) in a way that is bearable to the wounded eyes of the mourner. A Pre-Raphaelite lyricism and brightness of pictorial colour stylize the emotion, coding it in a system of coloration that is at once mannered and meaningful. Again, the manuscript provides clues as to how the Elysian vision bears upon reality. It explains that the fields are 'purple' because they are distant (p. 303), a gloss that might appear over-obvious to the reader – and must have struck the author in revision in this light – unless one is alert to the stress that is put on distance in Part Three as the measure of accommodation to great pain. 'So much depends . . .,' as Lily later murmurs to herself, 'upon distance' (pp. 176–7). Looking out to sea, she seeks to recast the vision:

making hillocks of the blue bars of the waves, and stony fields of the purpler spaces. Again she was roused as usual by something incongruous. There was a brown spot in the middle of the bay. It was a boat . . . Mr Ramsay's boat . . . (p. 168)

Blue . . . *purple* . . . *brown*: the colour-progression is a sequence of guides to demarcate distances; and the attainment of distance through strides of eyesight that focus and refocus the image one stage at a time further out is the novel's sole aim from this point. The superimposition of the purple vista of Mrs Ramsay's withdrawal upon the blue-and-purple expanses of sea over which Mr Ramsay recedes at once distinguishes them (the one is 'real', the other not) and integrates them, as they journey toward their places of rest. The remainder of the section is confined to calculation of apparent distances and the spatial relations between the boat, the cliffs, the steamers out to sea, the lighthouse, and the mind of Lily whose task it is to connect all of these phenomena so that she may make personal sense of the 'secret messages' they seem to signal to one another through the morning haze. As the lens of her eye focuses Mrs Ramsay as mortal goddess, so it projects Mr Ramsay toward impersonality, as her way of thinking of him takes on the formulaic terms in which ancient epic figures its heroes. Moving out to sea he is not invoked as 'Mr Ramsay', but archetypally as 'that very old man' (p. 169), nearing the threshold and horizon of life, a status which was intrinsic to the figure in its first conception (the novel being provisionally titled 'The Old Man' when the theme began to grip her imagination during the writing of *Mrs Dalloway* [see *Diary*, II, p. 317]).

In *Mrs Dalloway* the debt to past elegies in the tradition is frank and self-declaring. The refrain which bids itself accept a narrow, asexual, brief and trivial round of social activity in lieu of life goes to a tranquillizing rhythm of a sewing needle passing in and out of cloth: 'Fear no more, says the heart. Fear no more, says the heart' (p. 45) and concludes with the embrace of a life too inert to dare even the positive action of suicide: 'Fear no more the heat of the sun. She must go back to them' (p. 206). Unlike *To the Lighthouse*, the dead the novel mourns are the living: the insistent appeal to the dirge in *Cymbeline* (see p. 102) laments the fear of the sun itself, the sexual terror that runs for cover to the quiet consummation of an attic room where the sheet is stretched and the single bed narrow (pp. 52–3). In an earlier version of the Mrs Dalloway story, a further controlling text had been Shelley's *Adonais*:

And now can never mourn – how did it go? – a head grown grey . . . From the contagion of the world's slow stain . . . have drunk their cups a round or two before . . . From the contagion of the world's slow stain! She held herself upright.
 But how Jack would have shouted! Quoting Shelley, in Piccadilly! ('Mrs Dalloway in Bond Street' [1923], *Complete Shorter Fiction*, p. 148)

> From the contagion of the world's slow stain
> He is secure, and now can never mourn
> A heart grown cold, a head grown gray in vain . . .
> (*Adonais*, 40, lines 356–8)

Shelley's Platonist identification of the soul's incorporation in Time as a mortal stain which condemns youthful perfection to deterioration occurs at the poem's *peripeteia*, initiating the final Consolation ('He lives, he wakes . . . Mourn not for Adonais' [41, 361–2], the recognition of Adonais as *genius loci* ('He is made one with Nature' [42, 370]) and the transference of the poet's mantle. If Adonais is happily alive with the immortals, then Mrs Dalloway 'Quoting Shelley in Piccadilly' must be understood to number amongst the walking dead. The previous year Virginia Woolf had published T. S. Eliot's Dantean vision of spectral Londoners innumerably streaming through the metropolis:

> Unreal City
> Under the brown fog of a winter dawn,
> A crowd flowed over London Bridge, so many,
> I had not thought death had undone so many.
> (*The Waste Land*, I. 60–2)

She had the oddest sense of being herself invisible; unseen; unknown; there being no more marrying, no more having of children now, but only this astonishing and rather solemn progress with the rest of them, up Bond Street, this being Mrs Dalloway; not even Clarissa any more; this being Mrs Dalloway. (*Mrs Dalloway*, p. 13)

The intoning of the *Cymbeline* dirge – *no more . . . no more . . . any more* – takes on a depressive mood which extends throughout the final draft of *Mrs Dalloway*, for being uprooted from Shakespeare's bitter-sweet pastoral-elegiac context in the Welsh countryside and transferred to a modern urban landscape traversed by swarming anonymities of which Clarissa constitutes a soulless, nameless unit, travelling down the dying fall of the sentence's listless repetition of her social identification: *this being Mrs Dalloway . . . this being Mrs Dalloway.* When we turn from *Mrs Dalloway*, so profoundly nuanced by the elegiac tradition and offering these textual precedents as explicit (if ironic) keys to its own interpretation, *To the Lighthouse*, though it remembers a whole library of books by allusion, is veiled and gloved as it steals the emotions of a lifetime's passionate reading and makes them its own. From an urban appropriation of pastoral (itself a contradiction in terms) it returns to a pastoral setting. The dying fall of *Mrs Dalloway* is replaced by a life-affirming vigour even in the midst of loss and solitude, realized both in characterization and in the wit and freedom of the writing, what she called her 'quick and flourishing attack' (*Diary*, III p. 39). The death-wish still undeniably present in *To the Lighthouse* is arrayed against a world of fertility – its garden full of many children, its fish-teeming seas, a woman with an easel and paints, all summed up perhaps in Mr Bankes's memory of the presidential 'hen, straddling her wings out in protection of a covey of little chicks' on the road (p. 24). *To the Lighthouse* is a more positive elegy for demonstrating that it has so much to lose, its 'welter of children' (p. 25), full of 'wild and fierce' creatures like Cam, so nearly the human animal in a state of nature, who – 'No! no! no!' – would not give a flower to the gentleman. The novel celebrates in its first Part a natural abundance that calls to mind Milton's retelling of Genesis in Book VII of *Paradise Lost*, whose 'fry innumerable swarm' (400), birds' 'brood as numerous hatch, from the egg . . ./ Bursting with kindly rupture' (418–9) and nature 'teemed at a birth' (454). It is through the re-creation of the world of childhood in which the human, animal and green worlds have a happy nearness, which does not much trouble to designate the threshold between allowed and disallowed – the rough and tumble of the children registered by their mother's ears from first thing in the morning to last thing at night, the tramping in of the beach by the unwiped soles of offspring who bring the outside in, crabs, shells, reeds, stones – that the grief of the fall is generated with such poignancy. Where *Mrs Dalloway* broods on endings, *To the Lighthouse* recalls origins, and the magical terrain of childhood holiday – the idea of 'holiday' recalling its own source in 'holy day'.

Just as *To the Lighthouse* returns author and reader to youthful origins in close affinity to a garden- and sea-shore-world of nature, so the mode of the work frequently returns the elegy-form to its earliest origins in the Greek tradition. In the mourning central Part, especially as the cycle of destruction, turning through its meridian, casts forth intimations of resurgent power of hope, this 'Greek' allegiance seems especially potent. Renovating, semi-mythologized figures begin to surface (principally, Mrs McNab and Mr Carmichael), arbiters of some mysterious power – the numinous 'something', 'it', 'life' which the text cannot adequately focus in language. At the same time, the calamitous powers which in 'Time Passes' have collaborated to bring the house to the condition of ruin are refocused through a shift of mood to discharge energies into the novel which are exultantly at odds with the downward tenor of the requiem. The return to the earliest roots of pastoral releases this burst of new life:

Let the wind blow; let the poppy seed itself and the carnation mate with the cabbage. Let the swallow build in the drawing-room; and the thistle thrust aside the tiles . . . (p. 128; and see pp. 21–2)

> '*May violets grow on thistles,*
> *may they grow on thorns!*
> *May narcissus grow on juniper!*
> *The world must change.*
> *Daphnis dies! Pears grow on pine trees!*
> *Now the deer must chase the hounds,*
> *and the screech-owl's song sound sweeter*
> *than the nightingale's!*'
> (Theocritus, 'Thyrsis' Lament for Daphnis',
> *Greek Pastoral Poetry*, p. 50)

Two thousand, two hundred years separate the two texts; but nothing separates the emotion. The lamentatory murmur of the preceding lines ceases before the onset of a wild dance in which the elegist with cold mirth joins in the process of dereliction, voluntarily expropriating the self which has already been so nearly dispossessed. A bastard kind of liberty is inaugurated and praised, in which old values and securing expectations are abdicated now that they have been shown to offer no real accommodation to human need. 'Nature' as a fit haven for man has been subjected to question and found wanting; pastoral elegy condemns pastoral itself in offering a false order, and lets in a new kind of bizarrely recrudescent Nature whose comic grafting together of antipathies (Virginia Woolf's carnation–cabbage, Theocritus' pine-tree-pears) releases the elegist from the deadly inbreeding of self-tormenting emotion. Virginia Woolf's elaboration of this motif is toward a prodigal mingling of the outdoor and indoor worlds. As Mr Ramsay in a tantrum sends a plate spinning out of the window, so now the narrative voice cannot refrain from ejecting the contents of the domestic world literally out of its window, decorative china finding a natural home amongst the grass and wild berries with whose designs it is perhaps painted, and the chintz patternings of the armchair becoming a lure for butterflies seeking nectar in an hallucinatory floral garden. It is impossible to ignore the relish with which the text contemplates these developments: just as there is a certain natural justice in the idea of the deer turning on the hounds, so there is a pleasure both recidivist and anticipatory in the abolition of the constraints of the human dwelling-place:

In the ruined room, picnickers would have lit their kettles; lovers sought shelter there, lying on the bare boards; and the shepherd stored his dinner on the bricks; and the tramp slept with his coat round him to ward off the cold. Then the roof would have fallen; briars and hemlocks would have blotted out path, step, and window; would have grown, unequally but lustily over the mound, until some trespasser, losing his way, could have told only by a red-hot poker among the nettles, or a scrap of china in the hemlock, that here once someone had lived; there had been a house. (p. 129)

The picture conjured here is a pleasant reassertion of pastoral. As the house becomes decivilized, and unlivable to the upper middle-class genteel family of intellectuals, so it opens its doors to an illegitimate miscellany of trespassers. The passage includes one of the very few images of happy and enjoying sexuality to be found in any of Virginia

Woolf's works – the lovers who find haven 'lying on the bare boards', the deliciously unfelt discomfort being intrinsic to the English tradition of pastoral realism, the chilly forest of Arden in *As You Like It*, the 'drery ysicles' on the pastoral bough of Spenser's *Januarye* (*Shepheardes Calender*, I. 36). The images of the picnickers with their kettles and the lovers connote the Arcadian freedom of holiday; the shepherd, a Wordsworthian exponent of pastoral as a working life, decent, hard and pleasant by contrast to city life, and the tramp grateful for sanctuary from the weather redefine the structure of the house as a place of refuge. In its desecration, the temple ironically reachieves a holy use. In the final stage of decomposition, the house is given over to Nature's 'lustily' orgiastic growth, a reclamation of what man has appropriated by the principle of natural fecundity. And this would not after all have been so bad, the text signals: a new sort of liveliness and energy succeeds the human story. A single 'trespasser', visiting the ruin of the ruin like a vagrant rambler out of Wordsworth would pick up one or two clues, Mrs Ramsay's red-hot poker beaconing its cultivated message amongst the nettles, the potsherds, to indicate a human occupation of the site, of purely antiquarian interest. In the course of this section (penultimate in the central Part of the novel), the emotion has entirely modulated from dirge to fantasia, played *con brio*.

The 'force' which is brought in to work against this process of destruction-as-rebirth is equally focused as a deliverer of new life from the ruins of the old:

But there was a force working; something not highly conscious; something that leered, something that lurched; something not inspired to go about its work with dignified ritual or solemn chanting. Mrs McNab groaned; Mrs Bast creaked. They were old; they were stiff; their legs ached. They came with their brooms and pails at last; they got to work ... Slowly and painfully, with broom and pail, mopping, scouring, Mrs McNab, Mrs Bast stayed the corruption and the rot; rescued from the pool of Time that was fast closing over them now a basin, now a cupboard; fetched up from oblivion all the Waverley novels and a tea-set one morning ... (p. 129)

Whereas the picture of the open invitation extended by the overgrown ruin whose *locus amoenus* does not distinguish social categories was dominated by a lyrical flight in the future perfect conditional tense, the mopping-up operations of the cleaning ladies are set forth in a business-like succession of short clauses detailing activities undertaken in methodical order. The person of Mrs McNab seems to have been conceived to fulfil the traditional role of consolatrix in pastoral elegy, an external voice which moves in to the mourning world with a remedial message. But she is presented as a comic and ridiculous modulation of this function, a restorer not on the level of elevated spirit but of human clay. The reader who is familiar with Virginia Woolf's diaries will find it hard to restrain amusement at the author's idealization of the activities of working-class women in the light of her voluble lamentations as an employer of such labour, which, of course, set her and her class free for the life of the mind:

This morning ruined by the tears & plaints of Lottie, who thinks her work too hard, & finally demanded higher wages, which she could easily get, & so could Nell. I lost my temper, & told her to get them then. Up came Nelly in a conciliatory mood regretting Lottie's outburst; though pointing out the hardships of our printing-room, so untidy – work endless; had meant to ask a rise in February – everyone's wages raised . . . (Wednesday 12 December 1917, *Diary*, I, p. 91)

She sobbed, repented, took back everything she'd said; told me . . . the more people we had & the more mess we made the better she liked it. She begged me not to tell anyone; she kissed me & went off, like a chastened child, leaving me with a mixture of pity & (I suppose) self complacency. The poor have no chance; no manners or self control to protect themselves with; we have a monopoly of all the generous feelings – (I daresay this isn't quite true; but there's some meaning in it . . .). (Thursday 13 December 1917, *Ibid.*, p. 91)

The social snobbery which often makes the tone of *Mrs Dalloway* suspect and to which objection has been taken in *To the Lighthouse* in the supercilious attitudes that are alleged to lurk unreproved in the text toward the shop-keeping-class Charles Tansley ('"My father is a chemist, Mrs Ramsay. He keeps a shop"' [p. 16]; 'and he would ask one, did one like his tie? God knows, said Rose, one did not' [p. 13]) is difficult to forgive in the Diary entries under 'servant problem'. But for Virginia Woolf the question of class has a cross-bias which opens all judgements and prejudices based on accidents of birth and upbringing to question, and radicalizes her own perception of a hierarchy of value. In her fiction, gender is also class. Power based on gender neutralizes or reverses power founded in inherited social advantage. Charles Tansley offers the perfect example of this principle. The lowest of the low in the couth Ramsay world where one's father was not a shop-keeper – the Leonard Bast, perhaps, of the Ramsay society – Charles Tansley becomes powerful and dominant when he speaks with the voice of male authority: Lily is still oppressed by an internalization of his derogatory 'Women can't write, women can't paint' ten years after the speaker has vanished from the novel (pp. 148–9). Seen from this perspective, conventional social distinctions lose all relevancy, and woman is identified with woman regardless of origins, with a common stigma and maternal inheritance to maintain. During the decade after the writing of *To the Lighthouse*, Virginia Woolf was to develop these ideas not only in *A Room of One's Own* (1929) which is still concerned with intellectual privilege but in the then unfashionable feminist anti-militarism of *Three Guineas* (1938), which is forty years before its time in its presentation of a case on behalf of womankind and its traditions against a warfaring male 'civilization'.

The figure of Mrs McNab whose mediatorial role is demonstrated by her confinement to the central Part, is what is left to cope with the wreckage of the human family world after the holocaust. She appears only when Mrs Ramsay has vanished, and, as caretaker of the vacated house in some sense stands in for the lost mother; it is through her second sight that we are able to see traces of Mrs Ramsay 'like a yellow beam or the circle at the end of a telescope' (p. 127) wandering the garden or straying over the wall. The figure is conceived as a bizarre grotesque whose assimilation to features of the non-human world in combination with elements of personification implies a symbolic or mythic 'force' rather than a specific personality; she is a comic embodiment of the emblem so dear to the Victorians, of Hope with her blindfold eyes (if Hope could see how things really are in the world, she could not continue hopeful) and her hands strumming the lyre (the sweet, lulling music produced by her state of mind). Virginia Woolf reverses the icon from lovely maiden to hideous crone; the gentle trance becomes a witless inability to register the evils of the world in a debilitating form; the lyre becomes the music-hall song she mumbles:

As she lurched (for she rolled like a ship at sea) and leered (for her eyes fell on nothing directly, but with a sidelong glance that deprecated the scorn and anger of the world – she was witless, she knew it), as she clutched the banisters and hauled herself upstairs and rolled from room to room, she sang. Rubbing the glass of the long looking-glass and leering sideways at her swinging figure a sound issued from her lips – something that had been gay twenty years before on the stage perhaps, had been hummed and danced to, but now, coming from the toothless, bonneted, care-taking woman, was robbed of meaning, was like the voice of witlessness, humour, persistency itself, trodden down but springing up again ... hobbled to her feet again, pulled herself up, and again with her sidelong leer which slipped and turned aside even from her own face, and her own sorrows, stood and gaped in the glass, aimlessly smiling ... as if, after all, she had her consolations, as if indeed there twined about her dirge some incorrigible hope. (pp. 121–2)

Lurched, leered, clutched, hauled, rolled, hobbled, pulled, slipped, gaped: verbs of violent, inchoate activity impel the veering, tacking passage that seems to twitch from clause to clause with graceless locomotion. Indeed there are too many verbs or verb-participles to be easily carried by the sentences, which therefore mime with a peculiar exactness the incongruity of the old woman's inability to co-ordinate body movements or focus her mind or eyes. Her convulsive entrance into the house is figured as the heeling of a ship on a heavy sea, so that as she enters the pathological hall of mirrors a reader's mental eye is tricked into seeing a distorted image which is a ship as well as a human being – a grotesque emanation from the strange sea-world 'out there' with which Part Two is concerned. As the section develops, its emblematic character becomes steadily more explicit, demonstrating the extent to which Modernism can function more as a technical camouflage for motifs as old as the hills but which are considered less than avant garde by the cultural élite, than as new clothes for new ideas. The prose which mythologizes the figure is willing to disclose its allegorical meanings to the reader ('the voice of witlessness, humour, persistency itself ... consolations ... incorrigible hope'). As the lowest common denominator of what constitutes the human, Mrs McNab has been flourishing for millennia amongst the downtrodden proletariat to whom no special light is given but which founds a source of hope in its own hardship and fortitude. Symbolically rather than allegorically, we are left free to note that the mirror has no power over Mrs McNab: when she looks in the mirror she is not voluntarily looking at herself. The abeyance of self-conscious ego in this figure gives the deathly plane of the mirror's eye nothing to work on. Like Wordsworth's 'Idiot Boy' or his 'Old Cumberland Beggar', the low status human being is exempt from the maladjustments caused by the fall; in the absence of highly developed consciousness, consciousness cannot in the very nature of things be stained by the impurities of knowledge.

In the final version of *To the Lighthouse*, Mrs McNab does not begin to emerge as a consolatory figure until near the half-way point of 'Time

Passes'. But the whole of Part Two underwent radical revision, and in the original manuscript, she is an intrinsic presence from the second Section, in which much of the material for Section Five originates. The casting of the figure as an emblem of Hope is both more expository and explicit in the first draft:

~~Mrs. MacNab~~ yet
the living with their mops and their dusters let issue on the grave of beauty, ~~a~~ this incongruous song of the twisted the crazed and the thwarted, who, one ~~would think~~ had no reason to desire life, no gift to bestow, or give to take; & yet . . . they let rise up intertwined ~~with the dirge &the elegy~~ itself an incorrigible hope . . . not founded on reason . . . on the dumb persistency of the fountain of life . . . for ~~strangely as~~ in her sidelong glance there was, account for it as one may, the forgiveness of an ~~compl~~ understanding mind (*Holograph Manuscript*, p. 164)

Three cancellations offer insight into the original conception of the figure. The first emphasized the genre to which Mrs McNab belongs – 'the dirge and the elegy' – and labels the character of the Hope she exemplifies as not only 'incorrigible' (which remains in the final version) but irrational. The second is the formulation of her character as 'the dumb persistency of the fountain of life', a mixed but emotive metaphor in the context of this novel, which is given more social focus in the final version as 'persistency itself, trodden down but springing up again'. In the original, the image of the fountain of life links the figure with the representation in Part One of Mrs Ramsay as the 'fountain and spray of life' (p. 38; see pp. 24 f.), and signals the continuation of the fresh life-giving water of the feminine into the new age and through the saline, corrosive waters which flow through 'Time Passes'. This overt label of Mrs McNab as consolatrix is withdrawn in the final version perhaps because it makes the spiritual victory (which is only falteringly and tentatively won, if at all, by the final page) look too easy. Similarly the phrase 'the forgiveness of an . . . understanding mind' is deleted. It bears allusion to the Solomonic wisdom: 'I am but a little child: I know not how to go out or come in . . . Give therefore thy servant an understanding heart . . .' (I Kings, 3:7,9), which precedes his famous Judgement, and the building of the Temple to house the Ark of the Covenant. In the final version, Virginia Woolf writes of Mrs McNab that 'she was witless, she knew it' (p. 125). The wisdom which empowered Solomon to reconstruct Israel and its sacred places was based on the Hebraic equivalent of the Socratic and Delphic insistence that the root of earthly wisdom is the knowledge that we know nothing; that self-knowledge must precede all other researches. Solomon's profound and touching humility is also a demonstration that he already possesses such wisdom: he knows instinctively what he must ask for. In Virginia Woolf, the role of rebuilder of the ransacked sacred places is allocated to the servant class, 'nothing but a mat for kings & kaisers to tread on' (*Holograph Manuscript*, p. 165), one who lies so low to the earth as to be entirely passive and unimplicated in the passage of history. Buried in the troubled and problematic hope that is generated in Part Two to link the new world with the old we can guess out a much-camouflaged network of allusion to the regenerative promises of the Scriptures, from the wise humility of Solomon's request, to the Beatitudes ('Blessed are the poor in spirit'), and the icon of Christ as Suffering Servant. In the final version, the author has cut out many of the allusive filaments which lead down to interpretative sources beyond the work itself, simultaneously freeing and feminizing its mythological basis.

In Forster's *Howard's End*, in which a parallel cluster of motifs may be distinguished – the mother–daughter relationship between Mrs Wilcox and Margaret Schlegel reproducing the Demeter–Persephone duality as a centre of value and a controlling structure; a pastoral (and in the case of Forster georgic) family house and traditions moving down the generations – there is a mediating figure of an old woman, Miss Avery, who acts as caretaker of the house during Mrs Wilcox's absence and who ritually welcomes Margaret as the second Mrs Wilcox into her natural and mysterious inheritance (pp. 252–3). This cryptic figure is both chthonic and sibylline: her invocation signals the mergence of Margaret into the dead Mrs Wilcox and the inauguration of a line in which male inheritance is outlawed or marginalized (in the corn-goddess's world the males tend to suffer from hay fever [p. 255] and there is little use for them). The text treats her as a witch-like figure or crone, with supernatural powers of divination, a witness in language to the things that lie beyond it, a caretaker on the threshold of mortal and immortal realms. Like Mrs McNab in *To the Lighthouse*, Miss Avery is generally considered to be mad: Margaret pities her 'poor decaying brain' (p. 253) but grows to read 'the kink in her brain' as belonging to 'no maundering old woman' but to an alternative form of knowing (p. 254). Virginia Woolf was severely critical of what she saw as Forster's incapacity to integrate realism and mysticism in his books and said of *Howard's End*: 'Elaboration, skill, wisdom, penetration, beauty – they are all there, but they lack fusion; they lack cohesion; the book as a whole lacks force' ('The Novels of E. M. Forster', *The Common Reader*, I, p. 348). A reader of her criticism of Forster, however, may feel that the not very polite dismissiveness with which she slights her friend reveals a rivalrous irritability, as if she has heard a heavy foot trespassing on her own territory. *To the Lighthouse* has much in common with its pre-war predecessor, too much perhaps for *amour propre* to acknowledge freely. In *To the Lighthouse* and in *Howard's End* the crone-figures impersonate the role of the third person of the Demeter triad, Hecate, reverenced by the Greeks as 'Lovely Hecate of the crossroads' (*Orphic Hymn to Hecate*, 1) – the crossroads symbolizing the thresholds of birth and death over which she presides as mediatorial figure. The corn-goddess's messenger and companion, she aids and joins the reunion of mother and maiden in the harvest, completing the threefold motion of the moon (waxing, full, waning), the three ages of woman (maiden, mother, crone) and the cycle of the seasons. She is a midwife figure, bearing the occult secrets of female lore (in Christianity her name became synonymous with witchcraft). In *To the Lighthouse*, the archetype is cunningly bent and distorted by the author so as to refract it through the lens of the nightmarish vision of Part Two's combination of realism and the ghoulish incongruity of the speeding apocalyptic clock that times the narrative voice's acute distress. Realism equips Mrs McNab with broom and buckets; it diagnoses arthritis in every joint; it endows her with a history of sitting in the pub and hints at sexual irregularities in her earlier life. The fish-eye lens dilates the whole image into a reeling derangement of the human form invested with as little reason as the 'amorphous bulks' of the leviathan waves which 'lunged and plunged in the darkness or the daylight' (p. 125). The symbolic and mythic meanings associated with the Hecate figure are accommodated by these surrealist and realist methods to a discreet, low-key alignment with the mediatorial figure. The floral association, with the deep emotional reverberations it has accrued ('Mrs McNab stooped and picked a bunch of flowers . . . She was fond of flowers. It was a pity to let them waste' [p. 126]) looks back to Mrs Ramsay's wistful 'Lily is so fond of flowers' (p. 97) and forward to the lament for Prue as the flower maiden: 'She had let the flowers fall from her basket . . . She let the flowers fall from her basket, scattered and tumbled them on to the grass and . . . went too. Down fields, across valleys, white, flower-strewn . . .' (p. 185), with its powerful recall of Shakespeare's 'O Proserpina!/ For the flowers now that frighted thou let'st fall/ From Dis's waggon' (*The Winter's Tale*, IV. iii. 116–18) and Milton's:

> fair field
> Of Enna, where Proserpine gathering flowers,
> Herself a fairer flower by gloomy Dis
> Was gathered, which cost Ceres all that pain
> To seek her through the world . . .
>
> (*Paradise Lost*, IV. 268–72)

This vast, inter-textual context for all language in *To the Lighthouse*, and especially language with such a rich history of connotation in terms of the novel's needs and queries, gives a peculiar status to certain phrases. It is not possible for the narrative voice to set down a mimesis of such apparently casual chat as the commonplace words 'She was fond of flowers. It was a pity to let them waste' without those words seeming to deepen, charged with connotation, fed by the root-system of symbolic suggestiveness that underlies the whole novel. In her last novel, *Between the Acts* (1939) Virginia Woolf would note the strange behaviour of ordinary words in certain atmospheres or situations: '"The nursery," said Mrs Swithin. Words raised themselves and became symbolical. "The cradle of our race," she seemed to say' (p. 56); 'Words this afternoon ceased to lie flat in the sentence. They rose, became menacing and shook their fists at you' (p. 47). This is a telling comment on her own artistic practice: adroitly manipulative linguistic pressures exerted on some reiterated key words or phrases from the whole body of words in the text seem to 'raise' those areas of creative excitement or doubt so that for the reader's eye they appear as if italicized or set in a different fount on the page. But this process takes place almost subliminally, distinguishing her method against, say, those of Hardy or Lawrence who advertise loudly the constellations of imagery and thought whose words will seem to reverberate on the page. In the crucible of disintegration, Virginia Woolf lodges a mediatorial figure camouflaged as part of the chaos but able to extract order through transformative association with myth: a 'rusty laborious birth' that reinstates culture from its recurrence to that other breeding-ground of nature. Mrs McNab delivers the book back into the hand of the reader, as a book, rather than as a receptacle for 'breeding pale mushrooms and secreting furtive spiders' (p. 130). The Persephone–Demeter–Hecate triad is associated in the novel's adaptation (authentic to the original myth) with the rule of law and culture, civil conversing and sociability, with hospitality as one of its highest manifestations. The host–guest relationship which dominates Part One and is reinstated in a modified form in Part Three is accorded by the novel a sacramental status in harmony with the Greek ethos given and received as a mutual trust which mirrors the tempered concord both of the social world and the cosmos as a whole. It is the loss of restraints, the chaos, raggedness and raw moody emotion left in the wake of the vanished mother that Part Three of *To the Lighthouse* regrets: the pantomimes of the ageing father left unreproved, the bitter fret of the children unmediated, and the anguished outburst from the most repressed and reticent of mortals left hanging in the air with no answer: '"Mrs Ramsay!" she said aloud, "Mrs Ramsay!" The tears ran down her face' (p. 167).

This is a powerful and climactic moment in the elegy. The novel interrupts its recessional to invoke the dead. It implores the gods; it lets out the primal cry that calls for mother. This invocatory moment, in articulating all the silent, cumulative pain that has built in Lily's solitary thought throughout the final Part of the novel, brings the emotion to a pitch of agitation which, in the moment of expression releases the tension. The childish shriek of honest-to-God need and pain acts as a purgative both to Lily and to the elegy as a whole, which is free to compose itself toward the final Consolation. None of this section (moving to and including the cry) is present in the first version of the original manuscript: it begins to appear in the second manuscript draft (*Holograph Manuscript*, pp. 301ff.) Instead there is a great deal of uncertain re-drafting and considerable material, later deleted, concerning Mr Carmichael, Lily's silent companion on the lawn, who 'had the appearance of some vast brute which is now ~~remembering &~~ has gorged itself & is now ruminating. The book which ... was his ... source of nourishment, lay fallen on the grass' (ibid., p. 276). In the assimilation of Mr Carmichael to extra-human phenomena (here down the Chain of Being to resemble the vast bulk of a ruminant beast, later [see p. 137] upward to identification with a bizarre sea god, ironically stylized by the narrative voice toward incongruity and attributed with a cryptic, unknowable air) the author is evidently applying a similar lens to that with which she skewed and distorted, and hence defended her mythologization of Mrs McNab as a mediatorial figure. Of all the characters in *To the Lighthouse*, Mr Carmichael is the only one to have defied assimilation into the flow of narrative consciousness. He is and remains an alien in the text, an island of self which gives out no testament of evidence by means of which he might subject himself to interpretation, whether that of the narrative voice, the characters or ourselves. He is a reader of books who cannot himself be read; a poet whose lines are never shown around. In the first Part Mr Carmichael remains uniquely immune to Mrs Ramsay's insinuations of sympathetic mastery into the lives revolving around her. Knowing that he does not like her, she respects him for it, despite seeing him 'wince' away (p. 41) and 'shrink' (p. 42) from her appropriative attentions. Mr Carmichael's resistance to Mrs Ramsay's magic bears silent witness to her vanities, or so she divines, turning what she interprets as his silent reproach back upon himself. But the narrative abstains from endorsing her explanation of his behaviour as somehow a product of the misery of an unhappy marriage: it notably leaves a gap in the communal stream of consciousness to stand for Mr Carmichael. The effect of this breaking of the continuum of standard narrative technique is complex, for it is registered in a reader, if at all, then subliminally, since one simply passes over the place where his consciousness should be, and it is only in the third Part, when Mr Carmichael is explicitly and recurrently denoted by his monolithic silence as an intensely significant part of the landscape of meaning, that we become aware of how little clue we have been given to the nature of his inner life. His resistance both to the narrative voice and to Mrs Ramsay's intrusive curiosity also acts, of course, to enhance the significance of his momentary genuflection to her by which he completes the chain of her power at the end of the dinner-party scene. Rising, and 'holding his table napkin so that it looked like a long white robe' (a priestly image, comically deflated), he chants the words of the poem 'Luriana Lurilee' and 'bowed to her as if he did her homage' (p. 103). This moment of surrender, however, is allowed to remain mysterious and fugitive: Mrs Ramsay can assign no reason to it, neither does the narrative voice intervene to account for his thought processes.

A double image accrues of Mr Carmichael as on the one hand a tedious, shambling example of edgy old-manliness, carping, exacting, always shut up in a book, and a very unlovely physical specimen; but on the other hand a being of unusual powers, able to repel the insurgences of the narrative voice which lifts the skin of its interrogatees and with a fine flow of surmise haunts their most private places. Because he so rarely moves, he assumes an iconic and hieratic posture; because he says almost nothing, his silence speaks. The place of silence, pauses and gaps between sections of utterance always exerted on Virginia Woolf a powerful fascination. We can see this echoed in the account of Lily's painting of the picture in Part Three:

And so pausing and so flickering, she attained a dancing rhythmical movement, as if the pauses were one part of the rhythm and the strokes another, and all were related . . . (p. 148)

Within the novel, the gap between objects, represented by the blank space between sections, enacts the pause as part of the total rhythm. Panning to and fro between island and lighthouse in Part Three, the text mimes its inquiry: how one mass, the shore, can be balanced and measured against another, using the field of vision as the significant silent space which is the focus of investigation. In considering the blank spaces as generators of meaning, the reader is naturally an important co-creator of significance, supplying connectives to the incongruent masses of the prose. For instance, when we read Cam's verdict, looking back to shore at the end of Section 4 that 'they have no suffering there . . .' (p. 158) and in the next Section see Lily looking back at the boat in the throes of her suffering, it is we who are left to mediate the gap between the two Sections; we are co-opted to wrestle with Lily's, Mrs Ramsay's and everyone's 'problem of space'. For Cam's vision, we are forced to acknowledge, couldn't be more wrong, except in so far as the shore world equals to her the past where 'they shall grow not old as we who are left grow old' – and the novel's children will not be seen by Lily to come home from the lighthouse on this side of Eternity. In that a character retains complete silence on these matters which in one way or another turn all the novel's persons, its narrative voice and its reader into fellow-agonists, the immunity of the incommunicado participant will make it appear as if he holds a secret not available to the many. To the end of her life, Virginia Woolf remained absorbed in the meaning that can be attributed to silence. In *Between the Acts* (whose very title signifies the interstice or pause between two events as the revised location of meaning), a gathering occurs at which the unsaid rivals the said for potency: Giles's 'silence made its contribution to talk'; Mrs Manresa 'led them down green glades into the heart of silence' (p. 40). In this last brave testament to terminal fear, all occurs in a context of suspended animation, the phoney war which lifts the lid on all communal assumptions, a nervy twitching-aside of conventions, especially those on which the novel itself is based: '"Thought without words . . . Can that be?"' (p. 44).

But in *To the Lighthouse* a quality of energy and vigour resides that has been lost in the last painful message at whose centre stand receptacles containing emptiness about which there is nothing to be said: the empty cot in the empty birth-chamber (pp. 55–6), the empty vase in the empty room:

Empty, empty, empty; silent, silent, silent. The room was a shell, singing of
what was before time was; a vase stood in the heart of the house, alabaster,
smooth, cold, holding the still, distilled essence of emptiness, silence. (p. 31)

In *To the Lighthouse* the nursery is still warm with nascent life in Part
One, and in Part Three the house is still noisily reverberant, even
though it is mainly a matter of plates whizzing from windows, doors
slamming and paternal groaning. Activated memory, which looks back
eagerly to the season of youthful hope when colour is most sensual and
Paradise only just lost, makes the novel swim in a mysterious element
of dream and myth, when hieroglyphic wisdom may be attributed to
silence. In the end, the elegy, with all its shades and terrors so ruthlessly
confessed, reads the world by the light of original hope:

Mrs Ramsay sat silent. She was glad, Lily thought, to rest in silence, uncom-
municative; to rest in the extreme obscurity of human relationships. Who knows
what we are, what we feel? Who knows even at the moment of intimacy, This is
knowledge? Aren't things spoilt then, Mrs Ramsay may have asked (it seemed to
have happened so often, this silence by her side) by saying them? Aren't we more
expressive thus? The moment at least seemed extraordinarily fertile. (p. 159–60)

Words betray us, but there is access to 'fertile' quiet. In the lee of the
remembered silences of Mrs Ramsay, Lily understands the pauses
between utterances to be intensely rich in meaning and in the capacity
to offer the healing of repose ('to *rest* in silence . . . to *rest* in . . .
obscurity'). Adjusted to this light, the silence that obtains after Mrs
Ramsay's life is complete may also be known as a form of 'silence by
her side'. Part Three dramatizes the difficult but healing process for the
mourner of learning to trust the universe to continue to internalize the
beloved person as part of its plenitude, as a silent and invisible presence
which somehow endures alongside oneself. The case of Mr Carmichael
in Part Three is somewhat different but it signals to the same end. His
silence throughout the closing sections of the novel is fundamental to
its closing-down mechanism. Just as Mr Ramsay journeying out to sea
and reading as he goes becomes more spectrally 'other', performing
that curious, arcane gesture as he 'raised his right hand mysteriously'
(p. 173), so Mr Carmichael impersonates the mute, hierophantic bearer
of secrets the text itself can consciously never know. Sunk in his chair
comatose, he assumes the aspect of a kind of funerary monster, grotesquely half alive in the world of Time, half surviving in an underworld
of words which are understood purely as silent communication: that is,
on-the-page and in-the-head, the place where all voices meet and become

indeterminately one – where my voice as I read her words becomes assimilated to that of Virginia Woolf's or Shakespeare's voice but is still experienced as part of my self, joining me to all other voices who have read or will read the text. Mrs Ramsay has been allowed to voice this concept at the culmination of Part One when, hearing poetry, 'the words seemed to be spoken by her own voice, outside her self' (p. 102). Literature, then, and especially poetry, the language of universal man, is presented as the one channel of unity and unanimity in human life, not through what it can teach us to do or feel but in its emancipation of the ego from its solitary and solipsistic prison cell, in the moment of reading. It is at this point in Part One that Augustus Carmichael is able to join, fleetingly, the unison of loving 'homage' to Mrs Ramsay (p. 103).

In the manuscript, the author says that his book 'gave off the incense of poetry ... fumes of words ... permeated ... the old man's brain' (*Holograph Manuscript*, p. 225). Lily's growing assuredness as *To the Lighthouse* moves toward its conclusion that somehow the silent and impenetrable old man is in tune with her thoughts, sharing her voyage, seems linked with his keeping of his own counsel in the reading and writing of poetry. Not divulged even to the limited degree of the other characters in the fatuities of small talk, he speaks only the inward language of the one voice that is shared with Virgil (Mr Carmichael's light outlived all others as he read on by candle-light into the dark central Section), Shakespeare and all who write or read that greater talk which is the distillation of language, Shelley's 'transmitted effluence' which 'cannot die' in *Adonais* (46, line 47). In keeping his peace, Mr Carmichael, sunk into himself on the lawn beside her, affords Lily a strangely companionate experience as well as a lesson in a kind of knowing which comes hard to the strenuously questing people in Virginia Woolf's fiction, who have to get 'in' to acquire what they recognize as knowledge, exercising a Keatsian negative capability to guess their way to the centre of an imagined identity. This also is the narrative voice's way of knowing. However, the novel recurrently casts doubt on whether such an enterprise is ever more than hallucinatory to the imaginer, Narcissus taking copious notes from his hall of distorting mirrors. Mr Carmichael, by resisting interrogation, maintains selfhood in the novel but aids inquiry by teaching the baffled questor to back away and be patient with what is given. His very bulk teaches Lily patience, that essential lesson of elegy as it moves toward patience with what must be borne ('Patience, good sir,/ Do not assist the storm' [*Pericles*, III. i. 19]). For this relationship too is valedictory:

135

... Mr Carmichael ... seemed (though they had not said a word all this time) to share her thoughts. And she would never see him again perhaps. He was growing old. Also, she remembered, smiling at the slipper that dangled from his foot, he was growing famous. People said that his poetry was 'so beautiful'. (p. 179)

The story was originally given the provisional title 'The Old Man', and Mr Carmichael fits the archetype as well as Mr Ramsay, who – sailing toward journey's end under the eye of Lily's counterpart, Cam – takes on a similar unconstruable and hieratic readerly role to that of Lily's companion. The touching detail about the slipper dangling from his foot (always, for Virginia Woolf, an emotional corrective, almost a code for human vulnerability) also looks back unobtrusively to the arrival of Lily and Mr Ramsay at the 'blessed island of good boots' (see pp. 97f.). But it is given to Mr Carmichael to carry a greater share of the archetype's association with Wisdom (Merlin, Solomon, Zarathustra) than Mr Ramsay, in whom annoying and lovable humanity predominates. In Lily's final assessment, it is important that she is aware that this is her final chance to know Mr Carmichael: he too is journeying west, in time if not in space, and although her surmise about his grief over the death of Andrew Ramsay is probably accurate, this only increases his privacy for it implies 'the love that dare not tell its name'.

They only mumbled at each other on staircases; they looked up at the sky and said it will be fine or it won't be fine. But this was one way of knowing people, she thought: to know the outline, not the detail, to sit in one's garden and look at the slopes of a hill running purple down into the distant heather. She knew him in that way. (pp. 179–80)

With this final, ghostly remembrance of Mr and Mrs Ramsay arguing about the weather – '"Yes, of course, if it's fine to-morrow" ... "But ... it won't be fine"' (p. 9) – there comes a sense of relief at having escaped the confines of family life with its compulsions and bottled or explosive emotions. This way of knowing is also a way of letting-be, letting-go, the necessary acquiescence in the state of things that cannot be altered. In the final Section of the book, there are three utterances, Lily's '"He must have reached it"', '"He has landed ... it is finished"', and Mr Carmichael's sole recorded utterance in the novel, '"They will have landed"' (p. 191), which is also the last word that is spoken aloud by any character. For Lily, this once-only breaking by Mr Carmichael of the surface of his trance into corroborative utterance acts as a validation that he has been companionate all along, sharing the troubled, wishful places of the mind in which she has needed to quest for bearings. In both the original and the final versions of the novel, he is recorded as coming up from underwater like a fabulous personage who has inhabited and survived with full benignity the place of drowning: the liquid field of vision which has preoccupied the text, figuring the subconscious world hoarding its mental contents, those strange fish which the novel seeks to trawl with a net of words: Mrs Ramsay's 'ripples and the reeds in it and the minnows balancing themselves and the sudden silent trout' (p. 99). For readers of the elegy the final words of verification come with the authority of an unknown voice to testify to the survivability of those waters. They are words of consummation, looking toward Lily's final 'it was finished' (p. 192), offered by one who bears incongruous likeness to 'an old pagan God, shaggy, with weeds in his hair and the trident (it was only a French novel) in his hand'. In the first version he came 'Surging up . . . like a river God' and grasps a staff, his benevolence being explicitly stated. The probable origin of this configuration is *Lycidas*:

> Next Camus, reverend sire, went footing slow,
> His mantle hairy, and his bonnet sedge,
> Inwrought with figures dim, and on the edge
> Like to that sanguine flower inscribed with woe.
>
> (103–6)

The god of the River Cam, associated with the Cambridge traditions of academic learning, speaks before the penultimate Consolation in *Lycidas*. But Camus is associated with bewilderment; Virginia Woolf's consolator stands to Lily in an attitude of compassion and fellow-feeling, rising in her consciousness to manifest himself as a gracious icon of assuaging benediction:

They had not needed to speak. They had been thinking the same things and he had answered her without her asking him anything. He stood there spreading his hands over all the weakness and suffering of mankind; she thought he was surveying, tolerantly, compassionately, their final destiny. Now he has crowned the occasion, she thought, when his hand slowly fell, as if she had seen him let fall from his great height a wreath of violets and asphodels which, fluttering slowly, lay at length upon the earth. (p. 191)

We do not mistake this lustral figure for a *deus ex machina* whose location in the objective universe makes sense of all and sets all to rights. On the contrary, the God that is created out of the figure of

Lily's companion is fabricated straight out of the clay of her own need; he projects her own capacity for wordless trust, so hard-won against the tyrannous oppression exerted by language over consciousness, her own coming-to-terms and her wish to share thoughts and friendship. His gesture of blessing (using the magical powers of the mind's eye to cast out a camera image upon the face of reality) mirrors Lily's own new power to bless. The fact that she can project, in these beautiful sentences, the balm of healing and healthful imagery demonstrates to us as readers the triumphant message of a pastoral relocated within the spirit (like Milton's 'paradise within thee, happier far' (*Paradise Lost*, XII. 587) that in the garden of the psyche dock leaves do grow alongside nettles. The mythologized Mr Carmichael represents Lily's final adjustment, laboured for with such discipline against the chaos of her own grief, to things-as-they-are. Both mourner and priestly figure, Mr Carmichael synthesizes Greek and Christian sacred iconography: the outspread hands remember the Christian God's pity for and identification with human affliction, as the Suffering Saviour on the cross and God the Father of his children. In Lily's mind, he lets fall violets (associated with the lost mother) and asphodel, the Greek immortal flower of Elysium; in the original, these flowers were poppies, associated with his drug addiction, and to the ancients sacred flowers of sleep, forgetfulness and narcotic visionariness – Demeter's flowers especially, since they grew amongst the maturing corn. In the final version, the flowers are woven as a wreath which 'flutters' to earth with ritual slowness. The laying of a wreath is both a final tribute and a saying of farewell to the dead. Lily turns from the past, commits herself to Time ('it would be destroyed. But what did that matter?' [p. 191]) and with a surge of newly risen life completes her picture.

5. Completion

How hard it is to make an end. *To the Lighthouse* is concerned with the difficulty of bringing our affairs to a conclusion, saying goodbye, signing off a work of art or a life – and yet how potently desirable too, to call our work complete or to reshelve the book amongst its fellows and turn away with the sense of the whole shape and meaning of the book held evanescently in the mind, to be possessed until it fades. The mind that shaped *To the Lighthouse* seems to her readers so acutely and wakefully conscious of the ramifying implications of the writer–reader relationship that the synchronous completion of Lily's picture and the author's novel also calls into the field of contemplation the reader's conclusion of his co-operative act:

With a sudden intensity, as if she saw it clear for a second, she drew a line there, in the centre. It was done; it was finished. Yes, she thought, laying down her brush in extreme fatigue, I have had my vision. (p. 192)

She was oppressed by the tyranny of Time, yet denied its omnipotence, calling Time an illusion and seeking means in her fiction – the famous parentheses of *To the Lighthouse*, cyclical patternings and choric reiterations, contempt for the pretensions of plot – to evade its insistences. To make an ending, however protractedly lingering the valediction, is to make an inevitable concession to Time: all births surrender the child to mortality and the self to a fresh sensation of houseless emptiness around which it takes time to shrink into accommodation. And yet in the moment of completion, the saying of 'I have had my vision' which the co-opted reader may go over as many times as he likes to take down the book from the shelf, there is an expansion of the originally time-bound act into an eternally synchronized fusion of mental processes. As she brought *To the Lighthouse* to its conclusion, (she was here within three days of writing the last word, 'vision') both the wonder and the regret of reaching the landing stage united in her mind to give a painfully surcharged emotion:

The blessed thing is coming to an [end] I say to myself with a groan. Its like some prolonged rather painful & yet exciting process of nature, which one desires inexpressibly to have over. Oh the relief of waking & thinking its done   the relief, & the disappointment, I suppose. (Monday 13 September 1926, *Diary*, III, p. 109)

Life without the novel would throw her back upon her self, that most spectral of companions, the indwelling presence and purpose of the novel evacuated. The self becomes an empty chamber again, with all the terror and foreboding implicit in that image for Virginia Woolf. The entry for the next day registers waves of desolation breaking upon her in the early hours of the morning: 'Oh its beginning its coming – the horror – physically like a painful wave swelling about the heart – tossing me up ... Children ... Failure failure' (p. 110). Two weeks later she records deep depression coming from a sensation of nothingness; the phrase 'Where there is nothing' keeps recurring in her mind as she sits at the dining table (p. 111). Years later, she was to recall the period in the wake of *To the Lighthouse*, when she had abdicated her authorship to join the novel's readers and critics, as a time in which suicide hovered as near at hand as at any other time in her life. The completion of the most seamlessly whole and passionately expressive of her novels was at once the longed-for consummation of her meaning and the first stage of an ironic re-enactment of that experience of primal loss which the novel in its role as elegy had worked to atone and exorcize.

Virginia Woolf's life must be read as rich in new beginnings. Her mind was busy with new projects as soon as she felt herself nearing the conclusion of each work: side-stories would begin to sprout from the parent work, a new idea would lodge itself in her mind. In this way it was possible to breed new spiritual children from that 'Failure failure' in the barren aftermath of composition. Just over four years after *To the Lighthouse*, she was completing *The Waves*:

Here in the few minutes that remain, I must record, heaven be praised, the end of The Waves. I wrote the words O Death fifteen minutes ago, having reeled across the last ten pages with some moments of such intensity & intoxication that I seemed only to stumble after my own voice, or almost, after some sort of speaker (as when I was mad). I was almost afraid, remembering the voices that used to fly ahead. Anyhow it is done; & I have been sitting these 15 minutes in a state of glory, & calm, & some tears ... How physical the sense of triumph & relief is! Whether good or bad, its done; & as I certainly felt at the end, not merely finished, but rounded off, completed, the thing stated – how hastily, how fragmentarily I know; but I mean that I have netted that fin in the waste of waters which appeared to me over the marshes out of my window at Rodmell when I was coming to an end of To the Lighthouse. (*Diary*, IV, p. 10)

The final phase of *To the Lighthouse* can be read with hindsight as the genesis of *The Waves*; and the reader of *To the Lighthouse* is alive to much in this passage that recalls poignantly the experience of reading the earlier novel. The Muse's dictation which had her reeling along behind the sound of her own voice like the Lorelei 'voices that used to fly ahead' reminds us of Lily's complaint about language following 'a voice which speaks too quickly to be taken down by one's pencil' (p. 27). The agony of mental pleasure at bringing the work to fruition recalls the major theme of consummation within *To the Lighthouse*: *it will end*, *it was finished*, *It is enough! it is enough!*, *He has landed . . . It is finished*, *They will have landed*, *It is done; it is finished* shared impersonally like a communal dream-speech between a chorus of characters. The remote, tantalizing image of the solitary fin of an unknown creature out in the 'waste of waters' witnessed by the equally solitary observer from her window is a haunting figure for the creative psyche scanning the wordless expanses of its own dilating interior for clues to its unconscious secrets. The sharing of the act of creation between author and reader so that we read as Mr Ramsay reads in a common voyage, we land when he does and it is only done, it is only finished when we, with the author and the character spell these words over, witness to Virginia Woolf's unique attentiveness both to the reader as the final factor in the making of a novel and to her holistic notion of a book as the sum of its pages and binding, the hand that drives the pen and the eye-beam of the reader whose creative light completes the message

CHESTER COLLEGE LIBRARY

Select Bibliography of Works Consulted in the Text

1. Writings by Virginia Woolf

Between the Acts (1941), Harmondsworth, 1978.

Collected Essays, ed. Leonard Woolf, 2 vols., London, 1966.

The Complete Shorter Fiction of Virginia Woolf, ed. Susan Dick, San Diego, New York and London, 1985.

The Diary of Virginia Woolf, ed. Anne Olivier Bell, 5 vols., London, 1977–84.

The Essays of Virginia Woolf, vol. 2, ed. Andrew McNeillie, San Diego, New York and London, 1987.

Jacob's Room (1922), Harmondsworth, 1965.

The Letters of Virginia Woolf, ed. N. Nicolson, with J. Trautmann, 6 vols., London, 1975–83.

Moments of Being: Unpublished Autobiographical Writings, ed. Jeanne Schulkind, Harmondsworth, 1978.

Mrs Dalloway (1925), Harmondsworth, 1964.

Orlando: A Biography (1928), Harmondsworth, 1942.

Virginia Woolf's Reading Notebooks, ed. Brenda R. Silver, Princeton, NJ, 1983.

A Room Of One's Own (1929), Harmondsworth, 1977.

Three Guineas (1938), Harmondsworth, 1973.

To the Lighthouse (1927), London, 1977.

To the Lighthouse: The Original Holograph Manuscript, transcribed and ed. Susan Dick, London, 1983.

The Voyage Out (1915), Harmondsworth, 1970.

The Waves (1931), Harmondsworth, 1951.

2. Writings by Others

Arnold, Matthew, *Poems*, ed. M. Allott and R. H. Super, Oxford and New York, 1986.

Beja, Morris, *Virginia Woolf: A Casebook*, London and Basingstoke, 1970.

Bell, Quentin, *Virginia Woolf: A Biography*, London, 1972.

Boswell, James, *Life of Dr Johnson*, ed. G. Birkbeck Hill, 6 vols., New York, 1910.

Brontë, Emily, *Wuthering Heights*, Harmondsworth, 1965.

Eliot, George, *Essays*, ed. Thomas Pinney, New York, and London, 1963.

    Middlemarch, Harmondsworth, 1965.

    The Mill on the Floss, Harmondsworth, 1979.

Select Bibliography of Works Consulted in the Text

Eliot, T. S., *Selected Poems*, London, 1954.

Forster, E. M., *Abinger Harvest*, London, 1936.
  Howard's End, Harmondsworth, 1941.
  A Passage to India, Harmondsworth, 1961.

Gordon, Lyndall, *Virginia Woolf: A Writer's Life*, Oxford and London, 1984.

Harrison, Jane Ellen, *Prolegomena to the Study of Greek Religion* (1903), New York, 1955.

Holden, Anthony (ed.), *Greek Pastoral Poetry*, Harmondsworth, 1974.

Hopkins, Gerard Manley, *Poems*, ed. Robert Bridges, London, New York and Toronto, 1930.

Keats, John, *Poems*, ed. J. E. Morpurgo, Harmondsworth, 1953.

Milton, John, *Poems*, ed. John Carey and Alastair Fowler, Oxford, 1968.

Owen, Wilfred, *Collected Poems*, ed. C. Day-Lewis, London, 1964.

Plato, *Phaedrus and Letters,* trs. W. Hamilton, Harmondsworth, 1973.
  Protagoras and Meno, trs. W. K. C. Guthrie, Harmondsworth, 1956.
  Republic, trs. F. M. Cornford, London, 1941.
  Symposium, trs. W. Hamilton, Harmondsworth, 1971.

Pope, Alexander, *Poems*, ed. John Butt, London, 1968.

Pound, Ezra, *Selected Poems*, London and Boston, 1975.

Schlack, B. A., *Continuing Presences: Virginia Woolf's Use of Literary Allusion*, Pennsylvania and London, 1979.

Shakespeare, William, *Complete Works*, ed. W. J. Craig, London, New York and Toronto, 1943.

Shelley, Percy Bysshe, *Selected Poems*, ed. Timothy Webb, London and Totowa, 1977.

Sidney, Sir Philip, 'A Defence of Poetry' in *Miscellaneous Prose*, ed. K. Duncan-Jones and J. Van Dorsten, Oxford, 1973.

Spalding, Frances, *Vanessa Bell*, London and Basingstoke, 1983.

Spenser, Edmund, *Poetical Works*, ed. J. C. Smith and E. de Selincourt, London, New York and Toronto, 1965.

Swift, Jonathan, *Gulliver's Travels and Other Writings*, ed. Louis L. Landa, London and Oxford, 1976.

Tennyson, Alfred, Lord, *Poems and Plays*, London, New York and Toronto, 1965.

Wordsworth, William, *Lyrical Ballads*, ed. R. L. Brett and A. R. Jones, London, 1965.

FOR THE BEST IN PAPERBACKS, LOOK FOR THE

In every corner of the world, on every subject under the sun, Penguin represents quality and variety – the very best in publishing today.

For complete information about books available from Penguin – including Puffins, Penguin Classics and Arkana – and how to order them, write to us at the appropriate address below. Please note that for copyright reasons the selection of books varies from country to country.

In the United Kingdom: Please write to *Dept E.P., Penguin Books Ltd, Harmondsworth, Middlesex, UB7 0DA.*

If you have any difficulty in obtaining a title, please send your order with the correct money, plus ten per cent for postage and packaging, to *PO Box No 11, West Drayton, Middlesex*

In the United States: Please write to *Dept BA, Penguin, 299 Murray Hill Parkway, East Rutherford, New Jersey 07073*

In Canada: Please write to *Penguin Books Canada Ltd, 2801 John Street, Markham, Ontario L3R 1B4*

In Australia: Please write to the *Marketing Department, Penguin Books Australia Ltd, P.O. Box 257, Ringwood, Victoria 3134*

In New Zealand: Please write to the *Marketing Department, Penguin Books (NZ) Ltd, Private Bag, Takapuna, Auckland 9*

In India: Please write to *Penguin Overseas Ltd, 706 Eros Apartments, 56 Nehru Place, New Delhi, 110019*

In the Netherlands: Please write to *Penguin Books Netherlands B.V., Postbus 195, NL–1380AD Weesp*

In West Germany: Please write to *Penguin Books Ltd, Friedrichstrasse 10–12, D–6000 Frankfurt/Main 1*

In Spain: Please write to *Alhambra Longman S.A., Fernandez de la Hoz 9, E–28010 Madrid*

In Italy: Please write to *Penguin Italia s.r.l., Via Como 4, I-20096 Pioltello (Milano)*

In France: Please write to *Penguin Books Ltd, 39 Rue de Montmorency, F-75003 Paris*

In Japan: Please write to *Longman Penguin Japan Co Ltd, Yamaguchi Building, 2–12–9 Kanda Jimbocho, Chiyoda-Ku, Tokyo 101*

FOR THE BEST IN PAPERBACKS, LOOK FOR THE

PENGUIN SELF-STARTERS

Self-Starters is a new series designed to help you develop skills and proficiency in the subject of your choice. Each book has been written by an expert and is suitable for school-leavers, students, those considering changing their career in mid-stream and all those who study at home.

Titles published or in preparation:

Accounting	Noel Trimming
Advertising	Michael Pollard
Basic Statistics	Peter Gwilliam
A Career in Banking	Sheila Black, John Brennan
Clear English	Vivian Summers
French	Anne Stevens
German	Anna Nyburg
Good Business Communication	Doris Wheatley
Marketing	Marsaili Cameron, Angela Rushton, David Carson
Nursing	David White
Personnel Management	J. D. Preston
Public Relations	Sheila Black, John Brennan
Public Speaking	Vivian Summers
Retailing	David Couch
Secretarial Skills	Gale Cornish, Charlotte Coudrille, Joan Lipkin-Edwardes
Starting a Business on a Shoestring	Michel Syrett, Chris Dunn
Understanding Data	Peter Sprent

FOR THE BEST IN PAPERBACKS, LOOK FOR THE

CLASSICS OF THE TWENTIETH CENTURY

The Age of Reason   Jean-Paul Sartre

The first part of Sartre's classic trilogy, set in the volatile Paris summer of 1938, is itself 'a dynamic, deeply disturbing novel' (Elizabeth Bowen) which tackles some of the major issues of our time.

Three Lives   Gertrude Stein

A turning point in American literature, these portraits of three women – thin, worn Anna, patient, gentle Lena and the complicated, intelligent Melanctha – represented in 1909 one of the pioneering examples of modernist writing.

Doctor Faustus   Thomas Mann

Perhaps the most convincing description of an artistic genius ever written, this portrait of the composer Leverkuhn is a classic statement of one of Mann's obsessive themes: the discord between genius and sanity.

The New Machiavelli   H. G. Wells

This autobiography of a man who has thrown up a glittering political career and marriage to go into exile with the woman he loves also contains an illuminating Introduction by Melvyn Bragg.

The Collected Poems of Stevie Smith

Amused, amusing and deliciously barbed, this volume includes many poems which dwell on death; as a whole, though, as this first complete edition in paperback makes clear, Smith's poetry affirms an irrepressible love of life.

Rhinoceros / The Chairs / The Lesson   Eugène Ionesco

Three great plays by the man who was one of the founders of what has come to be known as the Theatre of the Absurd.

FOR THE BEST IN PAPERBACKS, LOOK FOR THE

CLASSICS OF THE TWENTIETH CENTURY

Gertrude   Hermann Hesse

A sensitive young composer, the narrator is drawn to Gertrude through their mutual love of music. Gradually, he is engulfed by an enduring and hopeless passion for her. 'It would be a pity to miss this book – it has such a rare flavour of truth and simplicity' – Stevie Smith in the *Observer*

If It Die   André Gide

A masterpiece of French prose, *If It Die* is Gide's record of his childhood, his friendships, his travels, his sexual awakening and, above all, the search for truth which characterizes his whole life and all his writing.

Dark as the Grave wherein my Friend is Laid   Malcolm Lowry

A Dantean descent into hell, into the infernal landscape of Mexico, the same Mexico as Lowry's *Under the Volcano*, a country of mental terrors and spiritual chasms.

The Collected Short Stories   Katherine Mansfield

'She could discern in a trivial event or an insignificant person some moving revelation or motive or destiny . . . There is an abundance of that tender and delicate art which penetrates the appearances of life to discover the elusive causes of happiness and grief' – W. E. Williams in his Introduction to *The Garden Party and Other Stories*

Sanctuary   William Faulkner

Faulkner draws America's Deep South exactly as he saw it: seething with life and corruption; and *Sanctuary* asserts itself as a compulsive and unsparing vision of human nature.

The Expelled and Other Novellas   Samuel Beckett

Rich in verbal and situational humour, the four stories in this volume offer the reader a fascinating insight into Beckett's preoccupation with the helpless individual consciousness, a preoccupation which has remained constant throughout Beckett's work.

FOR THE BEST IN PAPERBACKS, LOOK FOR THE

PENGUIN CRITICAL STUDIES

Described by *The Times Educational Supplement* as 'admirable' and 'superb', Penguin Critical Studies is a specially developed series of critical essays on the major works of literature for use by students in universities, colleges and schools.

Titles published or in preparation:

Antony and Cleopatra	Kenneth Muir
As You Like It	Peter Reynolds
The Great Gatsby	Kathleen Parkinson
Jane Eyre	Susie Campbell
Mansfield Park	Isobel Armstrong
Return of the Native	J. Garver
Rosenkrantz and Guildenstern are Dead	Roger Sales
Shakespeare's History Plays	C. W. R. D. Moseley
The Tempest	Sandra Clark
Tennyson	Roger Ebbatson
A Winter's Tale	Christopher Hardman
The Miller's Tale	John Cunningham
The Waste Land	Stephen Coote
The Nun's Priest's Tale	Stephen Coote
King Lear	Kenneth Muir
Othello	Gāmini and Fenella Salgādo